"John Schwarz is a careful thinker, a lover of the faith, an equipper of the church. He has devoted himself to making an understanding of Christian Scripture and thoughts available on a broad scale. I am grateful for his work."

John Ortberg, teaching pastor,
Menlo Park Presbyterian Church

"John Schwarz writes as a layman, and he writes so that laypersons can understand. However, what he writes shows the result of serious biblical scholarship. This is a good read for those who want to know what the Bible is all about."

Tony Campolo, professor emeritus, Eastern University

"Both a guidebook for inquirers and beginners and a refresher course for the casual, this brief survey of the Christian Bible, Christian beliefs, Christian history, Christian living and Christianity alongside other faiths is a book that excels. Brisk, exact and user-friendly, it merits a very wide ministry and will bring clarity of focus wherever it goes."

J. I. Packer, professor of theology, Regent College

"*Living Faith* is an excellent road map for those starting out on the Christian journey. It is a good primer on the history of the Bible. It paints an excellent picture of the Big Story of God at work and shows how the different parts of the Bible fit together. I warmly recommend it to all who want to flesh out their understanding of what it means to be a follower of Christ."

Leighton Ford, president, Leighton Ford Ministries

"Concise, readable, fascinating, accurate and above all, compelling to believers and nonbelievers who know little of the Bible and the life in Christ. I want this book to be a companion to everyone who reads the Bible. Lay men and women will love this summary, because it opens doors of understanding."

Jerry E. White, president emeritus, The Navigators

"John Schwarz has written a reliable introduction to Christianity—simple but not simplistic, straightforward and brief."

Tim Stafford, senior writer, *Christianity Today*

"*Living Faith: A Guide to the Christian Life* by John Schwarz is a much-needed book that provides information to whet readers' appetites. It also opens wide the doors to help us see and imagine the future into which the Triune God is calling us even now."

Sara S. Henrich, associate professor of New Testament, Luther Seminary

"This primer is a must read for anyone who is looking for an informed overview of the Bible, Christian traditions and the continuing imperative for evangelism. Schwarz, long a lay teacher, provides an easy-to-read guide to basic facts, themes and dates pertaining not only to the foundation and development of the church but also to simple but important clues for living the Christian life amid the challenges of a confusing world. I highly recommend *Living Faith*!"

Cain Hope Felder, professor of New Testament language and literature, Howard University

LIVING FAITH

LIVING FAITH

A GUIDE TO THE CHRISTIAN LIFE

JOHN SCHWARZ

BakerBooks

Grand Rapids, Michigan

© 2005 by John Schwarz

Published by Baker Books
a division of Baker Publishing Group
P.O. Box 6287, Grand Rapids, MI 49516-6287

Printed in the United States of America

Library of Congress Cataloging-in-Publication Data
Schwarz, John Edward, 1931–
    Living faith : a guide to the Christian life / John Schwarz.
       p.   cm.
    ISBN 0-8010-6566-6 (pbk.)
    1. Christianity. I. Schwarz, John Edward, 1931– Handbook of the Christian faith. II. Title.
    BR121.3.S385 2005
    230—dc22   2004030878

Living Faith is an abridged version of *A Handbook of the Christian Faith* (Bethany House Publishers, 2004).

CONTENTS

FOREWORD

If you wanted to study ancient Tibetan architecture, you would sign on for a course, get the study materials and settle down to a regular pattern of reading, discussing, looking things up and steadily learning more and more. A great many people in today's world are used to the idea, if not the reality, of taking on a new subject and gradually making it their own.

But with Christianity it's different—or at least a lot of people think it is. In most Western countries, a great many people imagine they already know what Christianity is. Mention Jesus or God or Easter and they have at least a rough idea of a story of things happening long ago; a way of life involving prayer and some kind of holiness; attendance at religious ceremonies, especially church; and, of course, giving money. (There are quite a number of people in Western culture who don't know even this much, but they are not likely to be reading these words.) As far as most people are concerned, that's about it. There's nothing much more to be said. Even if they don't believe or practice the Christian faith, they know (so they imagine) what it's all about.

But they don't. With a very few exceptions, they know as little about Christianity as I do about Tibetan architecture. They don't know that Christianity began as a first-century Jewish messianic sect, at a time of great social and religious ferment. They don't know that there is excellent evidence to support the early Christian belief that Jesus really did rise from the dead. They have no idea that his first followers believed that world history had turned its great corner with that event and that they now were living in a world already transformed by God's love and waiting for its final deliverance from all evil and sorrow. They are blissfully unaware of the theological explosion in which, within a few short decades, the church explored in great and sophisticated detail its belief that Jesus himself was the personal presence of the one true God of Jewish monotheism and that his death had fulfilled the ancient prophecies about the One dying for the sins of the many. If such people think of the phrase "Holy Spirit," they probably don't have much idea to whom or what this might refer.

It doesn't stop there. It has never crossed the mind of the average person in the street that Christian faith has an inescapable political dimension, because Jesus' followers are committed to worshipping and serving him ahead of all others. And if they think of what Christians believe about the ultimate future, chances are the word *heaven* is as far as they'll get, without ever imagining that the New Testament speaks of new heavens *and a new earth*—and that this is why the resurrection of the body matters so much.

In other words, most people in our culture have no idea what a fascinating thing early Christianity was. And that includes most Christians today. But they need to know, and this book, *Living Faith: A Guide to the Christian Life* by John Schwarz, will help them get on board for the educational experience of a lifetime.

It doesn't stop there. Christianity didn't just explode into life and then stay exactly the same. Ever since the time of Jesus' first followers, subsequent Christian generations have explored different dimensions of what it means to follow Jesus, to find his life welling up within their own, to belong to the family we call the "church," stretching as it does across space and time and into extremely different cultures. Because Christians believe that the Holy Spirit has been guiding the church through the years (not that the church has always cooperated), what previous generations have written and done remains important to us today. But again, most people in our world, including most practicing Christians, don't know much about that. They need to know. And this book will help them get started.

In particular, though the average onlooker is correct to imagine that Christianity involves a particular lifestyle and certain practices, he or she doesn't have a clear idea of how it all ties together. What has baptism to do with the Christian view of marriage, or either with the Christian calling to be stewards of God's creation, or any of that to do with the service of Holy Communion? Why has Christianity generated such wonderful works of art, music and literature? What does Christianity have to say about prayer, beauty, suffering and different kinds of religious faith? Why should Christians be particularly concerned to look after their neighbors in the global village? Why should they bother themselves with questions about world poverty, AIDS, the problem of third-world debt or international terrorism? All this seems a confused jumble to many people. But the Christian vision of reality makes sense of it all, and even a small amount of study will put you on the way to understanding how it works.

This little book offers a good overview of the Bible and the biblical story. It also provides a brief sketch of the history of Christianity, sets forth important Christian beliefs, shows the uniqueness of Christianity vis-à-vis other religions, suggests ways for Christians to deepen their faith through prayer and study and, last, offers some guidelines for Christian living. For those who are serious about their faith and the desire to understand it better, this book is a good place to begin. It is not the last word on any of the subjects it covers, but for many people it may be a first word. My hope and prayer is that through this book you will not only learn a great deal, but that you will be brought to hear and understand the living Word of God more fully for yourself.

Tom Wright
Bishop of Durham, England

1

THE STORY AND MESSAGE
OF THE BIBLE

It is said that religion is humankind's attempt to reach God and that Judaism and Christianity are God's attempt to reach humankind. He does this through *general* and *special* revelation. *General revelation* refers to God's creation of the "heavens and the earth" (creation implies a Creator). *Special revelation* refers to God's "words" to the patriarchs and prophets of Israel and to the apostles of Jesus and to God's saving acts in the exodus and Jesus' death and resurrection. The Bible is the inspired, written testimony to God's special revelations.

The English word *Bible* comes from the Greek word *biblia*, meaning "books." The books in the *canon*—those books that were accepted by the rabbis and church fathers as Holy Scripture—were written over a twelve-hundred-year period, from 1100 B.C. to A.D. 100. They were written by more than forty different authors, some of whom are known but most of whom are not, from places like Jerusalem and Babylon in the Old Testament and Corinth and Rome in the New Testament.

The word *testament* comes from the Latin *testamentum*, meaning "oath" or "covenant." The Old Testament contains the covenant that God made with Israel at Mount Sinai when he said, "If you obey me fully and keep my *covenant*" (Exod. 19:5 NIV, emphasis added). The New Testament contains the covenant foretold by the prophet Jeremiah when he said, "'The time is coming,' declares the LORD, 'when I will make a *new* covenant'" (Jer. 31:31 NIV, emphasis added). Jesus instituted this covenant at the Last Supper when he told his disciples, "This cup is the *new covenant* in my blood" (Luke 22:20, emphasis added).

The Old Testament Canon

The Old Testament has thirty-nine books in Protestant Bibles, forty-six books in Catholic Bibles (the additional books come from the *Septuagint*) and fifty books in Eastern Orthodox Bibles (the Catholic Old Testament plus 1 Esdras, 3 Maccabees, the Prayer of Manasseh and Psalm 151).

- The *Torah* or *Pentateuch* comprises the books of Genesis, Exodus, Leviticus, Numbers and Deuteronomy. In the Pentateuch, God calls (elects) Abraham to be the father of Israel, frees the Israelites from their bondage in Egypt and enters into a covenant with Israel at Mount Sinai.
- The *Historical Books* are the books of Joshua, Judges, Ruth, 1 and 2 Samuel, 1 and 2 Kings, 1 and 2 Chronicles, Ezra, Nehemiah and Esther. These books cover the eight-hundred-year history

of Israel, from its entry into the Promised Land (Canaan) under Joshua around the year 1250 B.C., to the return of the exiles from their captivity in Babylon in 538 B.C., to the rebuilding of Jerusalem in the early 500s B.C. and the "restoration" of Jewish life in the mid-400s B.C.

- The *Prophetic Books* are the collected writings of the four major or longer prophets—Isaiah, Jeremiah (and his Lamentations over the fall of Jerusalem), Ezekiel and Daniel—and the twelve minor or shorter prophets—Hosea, Joel, Amos, Obadiah, Jonah, Micah, Nahum, Habakkuk, Zephaniah, Haggai, Zechariah and Malachi. The Hebrew Bible calls the minor prophets The Book of the Twelve.

- The *Writings*, which Christian Bibles call the devotional and wisdom literature, are the books of Job, Psalms, Proverbs, Ecclesiastes and the Song of Solomon.

The Apocrypha

The Greek translation of the Old Testament is called the *Septuagint*. According to Jewish legend, seventy-two elders and scribes (six from each of the twelve tribes) went to Alexandria, Egypt, in approximately 250 B.C. and translated the Hebrew Scriptures into Greek so they could be read by Jews living outside Palestine. (*Septuagint* comes from *septuaginta*, Latin for seventy, the nearest round number for the seventy-two translators.) The Septuagint includes fifteen books that are not in the Hebrew Bible, books like Tobit, Judith, 1 and 2 Maccabees and Baruch. When Jerome completed his translation of the Hebrew Scriptures into Latin in 405, he included several of these books, with a caution from the rabbis with whom he worked that these books should not be considered to be on the same level as the books in the Hebrew canon. Over time these *deuterocanonical* ("second canon") books were accepted by the church; at the Council of Trent (1545–1563), the Roman Catholic Church gave them equal status with the books in the Hebrew canon.

But when Martin Luther and the Reformers translated the Bible into German and other languages, they either omitted these books or put them in a separate section called the *Apocrypha*, from a Greek word meaning writings of questionable authorship or authenticity, because they had not been received into the Hebrew canon.

Deuterocanonical books like 1 and 2 Maccabees shed light on the years between the two Testaments; other books let us see the development of Jewish thinking regarding the afterlife, which is only briefly alluded to in the Hebrew Scriptures.

The New Testament Canon

The New Testament has twenty-seven books, which are also divided into four sections.

- The *Gospels* of Matthew, Mark, Luke and John are the written testimonies to the life, death, resurrection and promises of Jesus.
- The *Acts of the Apostles* is the story of the early church in Jerusalem and Paul's missionary travels and journey to Rome, covering the period A.D. 30 to 60.
- The *Letters* and *Epistles* comprise Paul's nine church letters (Romans, 1 and 2 Corinthians, Galatians, Ephesians, Philippians, Colossians and 1 and 2 Thessalonians) and four personal letters (1 and 2 Timo-

thy, Titus and Philemon); the anonymous letter to the Hebrews; and the seven so-called general letters (James; 1 and 2 Peter; 1, 2 and 3 John; and Jude).

• The book of *Revelation* contains John's apocalyptic visions of the sovereignty of God and his coming triumph over the forces of evil.

The New Testament Books: Order, Acceptance and Authenticity

In the Old Testament, the books appear more or less in chronological order. This is not true in the New Testament. Paul, who was martyred in Rome in the mid-60s, wrote all of his letters before any of the Gospels, the first of which, many scholars believe, was written around the year 70, and also before the book of Acts, which narrates Paul's travels. Further, the letters of Paul are ordered according to length, not date—Romans, the longest Pauline letter, is first in line, though it was one of Paul's later letters. And though Matthew has pride of place among the Gospels, most scholars today believe that Mark was the first Gospel to be written.

The basis on which books were accepted into the New Testament canon was threefold. First, the author had to have been an apostle or a disciple of an apostle, like Mark with Peter and Luke with Paul. Second, the book had to be consistent with the church's overall teachings. Third, the book had to have enjoyed churchwide acceptance and usage.

Christians have good reason to be confident of the New Testament's reliability and authenticity. More than five thousand Greek manuscripts of the Scriptures have been found and cataloged, including complete manuscripts dating from the mid-300s, such as the *Codex*

Sinaiticus (discovered at Mount Sinai in 1844 and now in the British Museum in London) and the *Codex Vaticanus* (now in the Vatican Library in Rome). Also, the books in the New Testament were written within a generation or two of Jesus' death. This contrasts with the miniscule number and late dating of the writings of Plato, Aristotle, Julius Caesar and others in antiquity, which scholars universally accept as authentic. British scholar John A. T. Robinson, in his book *Can We Trust the New Testament?*, calls the New Testament "the best-attested text of any writing in the ancient world."

The Gospels: The Center of the New Testament

The central narrative of the New Testament is the public ministry, salvational death and bodily resurrection of Jesus of Nazareth. This narrative is contained in the four Gospels. Some ask why there are four Gospels rather than one; others ask why there are *only* four Gospels, because there were "gospels" other than those that made their way into the New Testament, some two dozen in all, such as the gospel of Peter, the gospel of Thomas and the gospel of Philip. With regard to this question, the gospels that did not make it into the canon were judged by the early church fathers to not have been apostolic in origin or accepted by the church at large.

As to why there are four Gospels and not one, the church fathers felt that our understanding of Jesus would be richer and deeper with all four rather than with only one or with a harmonized gospel such as Tatian's *Diatessaron* ("fourfold"), which appeared in the latter half of the second century and remained popular for many years. The fact that Tatian chose the four canonical Gospels as the basis for his composite gospel testifies to the widespread acceptance of Matthew, Mark, Luke and John over any of the rival gospels that were then beginning to circulate.

The Theme of the Bible

Most scholars believe the Bible has an overall unifying theme. Some say the theme is that of *covenant*—the covenants that God made with Israel and through Jesus with all of humankind. Others say the theme is *salvation history*—the successive, progressive revelations of God so that all might come to the knowledge of the truth and be saved. Still others say the theme is *promise and fulfillment*—God's promise to David that from his descendants would come one whose "throne shall be established for ever" (2 Sam. 7:16) and the fulfillment of this promise in Jesus, who was from the line of David and who the angel Gabriel told Mary would inherit "the throne of his ancestor David" (Luke 1:32).

The central truth claims of Christianity are that Jesus was God incarnate, that he died a substitutionary death to rightly relate us to God and that he was raised from the dead to confirm his divine mission. Is there any evidence that Jesus rose from the dead? The surest evidence is the witness of those who were martyred for their faith. Why is this evidence? Because, as Paul Little says in his book *Know What You Believe*, "People will die for what they *believe* is true, but no one willingly dies [as did Peter and Paul in Rome and others throughout the Roman Empire] for what they know is *false*" (emphasis added).

When Lord Nelson defeated the French fleet in the Battle of the Nile in 1798, he told the British Admiralty that *victory* was not a big enough word to describe what had taken place. When we talk about Jesus' victory over

19

death on Easter morning so that we may not perish but have eternal and everlasting life, *victory* is not a big enough word to describe what took place.

The Translations of the Bible

In Jesus' day, the Scriptures were scrolls, such as the Isaiah scroll that Jesus read in the synagogue at Nazareth (Luke 4:17–21). They were written on papyrus, a plant that grew along the Nile River; later on parchment, made from the skins of goats and sheep; and finally on paper. In the second century, Bibles were produced with pages that could be turned. With the invention of the printing press by Johann Gutenberg in 1456, the production of Bibles moved from handwriting to movable type.

The earliest Bibles were written in Greek. When the church moved west, there was need for an authoritative Latin translation, which was completed by Jerome, the most accomplished linguist of his day, in 405. Jerome's Bible came to be called the *Vulgate,* from a Latin word meaning "common" or "ordinary" language. The first translation of the Bible into English was completed by John Wycliffe in 1382. The *King James Bible* of 1611, authorized by King James of England (who reigned from 1603 to 1625), became *the* Protestant Bible of the English-speaking world until well into the twentieth century, and its popularity continues even today. The twentieth century saw more than one hundred new translations. Reasons for this included the discovery of new information about first-century Israel from archaeological finds, such as the Dead Sea Scrolls; the discovery of better manuscripts from which to translate, such as the *Codex Sinaiticus*; and the need to update certain words used in biblical translations, such as *Thee* and *Thou*, and to make the Bible more gender-inclusive.

Reading the Bible

The following are some "helps" in reading the Bible.

- The Bible should be read with an *open mind* and with the view and expectation that God *will speak* to us through his Word. It is said that the Bible is God's "telephone line" to us.
- The Bible is *one continuous story*, from Genesis to Revelation. The biblical story of salvation begins with God's call of Abraham and his covenants with Moses and David; it reaches its fulfillment in the death and resurrection of Jesus.
- The Bible was written several thousand years ago and is, in places, *hard to understand*. Don't be discouraged. Someone once asked William Booth, the founder of the Salvation Army, what he did when he came across something in the Bible he did not understand. Booth said, "I do the same thing I do when eating a fish: I put the bones on the side of the plate and get on with the good meat."
- The Bible should be read in its *plain* or *natural sense*, without veering off into extreme literalism. Also, be conscious that the Bible is really a "library," with books of history (Samuel, Kings, Chronicles, Acts), prophecy, poetry (like the Psalms), wisdom literature (Proverbs and James) and lots of letters.
- The Bible is its *own commentary*. This means that the New Testament interprets the Old Testament. When Jesus "declared all foods clean" in Mark 7:19, he overruled the laws regarding clean and unclean food in Leviticus 11.

Five Popular Bible Translations

The *New Revised Standard Version* (NRSV, 1989) is considered by many to be the most faithful rendering of the Greek text. It claims to be "as literal as possible, as free as necessary" (from the preface to the NRSV). *Today's English Version* (TEV, 1976) or the *Good News Bible* or *Good News Translation* (1992) is a sixth-grade reading level paraphrase rather than a word-for-word translation. The *New International Version* (NIV, 1984), the most popular Bible in terms of sales, is intentionally conservative and widely used by evangelicals. The *New Living Translation* (NLT, 1996) is a popular junior-high reading level "thought-for-thought" translation. *The Message* (2002) is a contemporary paraphrase that uses modern-day words and terms.

2

THE HEBREW SCRIPTURES

God entered into a covenant with Israel at Mount Sinai. Since Christians believe that God made a *new* covenant, which Jesus instituted at the Last Supper, they have traditionally referred to the covenant that God made with Israel as the *old* covenant. But if God made a new covenant, some ask, why bother reading the Old Testament? Because Jesus came to fulfill God's promises to Israel, which are recorded in the books of the Old Testament. God's plan of salvation did not begin with the birth of Jesus in Bethlehem; it began some two thousand years earlier with the call of Abraham in the Mesopotamian city of Ur.

The Pentateuch: Creation, Fall, Election and Covenant

The story of Israel becoming a nation is contained in the first five books of the Bible, which in the Jewish Scriptures are called the *Torah*, from the Hebrew word *tora*, meaning "instruction." In the Christian Old Testament they are called the *Pentateuch*, from the Greek words *penta* ("five") and *teukhos* ("scrolls"). The Pentateuch contains Israel's most important and sacred writings, those in which God chose or *elected* Israel to be his people (the covenant with Abraham), spoke to Israel's patriarchs and leaders (Abraham, Jacob, Joseph and Moses), rescued or *saved* Israel from its bondage in Egypt (the exodus) and entered into a *covenant* with Israel (the Mosaic Covenant). The Pentateuchal books are central to Jewish worship and are read aloud in their entirety each liturgical year. The five books are as follows.

- **Genesis:** The creation of the universe, the earth, vegetation, living creatures and humankind; the stories of Adam and Eve, Cain and Abel, Noah and the flood and the Tower of Babel; the call of Abraham to go to a new land; and the stories of Abraham, Isaac, Jacob and Joseph.
- **Exodus:** Israel's enslavement in Egypt; the birth and call of Moses; the ten plagues; the *exodus* ("going out") from Egypt; God's covenant with Israel at Mount Sinai; and the Ten Commandments.
- **Leviticus:** Levitical rules relating to religious offerings; clean (*kosher*) and unclean food; diseases, sexual relations and cleanliness; and *Yom Kippur*, the Day of Atonement, Israel's high holy day (Judaism's "Good Friday").

24

- **Numbers:** The census (numbering) and orga-
  nization of the twelve tribes of Israel into a community or nation; God's call to take possession
  of Canaan, the land promised to Abraham's descendants; and Israel's forty years in the Sinai
  desert as God's judgment for refusing to do so.
- **Deuteronomy:** The second (*deutero*) telling of
  Israel's story; the *Shema*, Israel's great confession of faith: "Hear, O Israel: The LORD our God,
  the LORD is one" (6:4 NIV); Moses' instructions
  to the twelve tribes before their invasion of Canaan under the leadership of Joshua; and Moses'
  death.

The Prologue

Genesis 1–11 is the story of the downward fall—Adam
and Eve's disobedience in the garden, Cain's murder
of Abel, God's displeasure with creation and the great
flood, and the Babylonian Tower of Babel. It is also an
answer to the question, "Why did God call Abraham?"
God called Abraham as the first step in his plan to rescue the human race. Why *Abraham*? According to later
rabbinic literature, God called many, but only Abraham
responded. The working out of God's plan of salvation
begins in Genesis 12 and continues through the rest
of the Old Testament and all the way to the end of the
New Testament.

Abraham: The Founding Father

The biblical story of salvation begins with the "call" of
Abraham (Gen. 12:1), whose descendants were to bring
God's blessings to "all the families of the earth" (Gen.

12:3). Abraham's wife Sarah is old and barren, but God's grace comes upon her, and she bears a son, who is named Isaac. God commands Abraham to sacrifice Isaac to test his loyalty and obedience (Genesis 22). Abraham proves faithful, and God instead provides a ram for the sacrifice. Isaac has twin sons, Esau and Jacob. The ancestral line continues through Jacob, whose name is changed to *Israel* by an angel of God (Gen. 32:28). Jacob's "sons" become the twelve tribes of Israel. Jacob's favorite son, Joseph, is sold into slavery by his jealous brothers; he later becomes the viceroy (second-ranking official) of Egypt. A famine in Canaan brings Jacob and his family to Egypt, where Joseph cares for them, after which they settle in Goshen in northern Egypt.

Moses: Deliverer and Lawgiver

Some six hundred years after Abraham, the Israelites find themselves living as slaves in Egypt. God hears their cries for help and calls Moses at a "burning bush" (a bush that burned but was not consumed) to lead the Israelites out of Egypt. The exodus—Israel's salvation from bondage in Egypt (c. 1290 B.C.)—is the single most important event in Israel's history. The story of the exodus is retold every year at Passover. It is the story of the angel of death who struck down the firstborn of the Egyptians but *passed over* the homes of the Israelites (Exodus 11–12). Moses led the Israelites out of Egypt and across the Sinai Peninsula to Mount Sinai, where God entered into a covenant with Israel (Exod. 19:3–6) and gave Moses the Ten Commandments.

God prepared Moses for his "calling." First, his early years with his mother, who was miraculously retained by Pharaoh's daughter to nurse and help raise her own child, made him aware of his Jewish heritage. Second, his education in Pharaoh's household prepared him to confront the Pharaoh when called by God to do so. Third, his years in the Midian desert (southeast of Sinai) enabled him to lead the Israelites through the desert to Mount Sinai, where they received God's law and commandments. It is said that the New Testament was written after the followers of Jesus had experienced the risen Christ—that is, from the other side of the cross. The same might be said of the Old Testament: it was written after the Israelites had experienced the God of Abraham, Isaac, and Jacob—that is, from the other side of the Red Sea.

The Historical Books: The Rise and Fall of Israel

The historical books trace the history of the Israelites in the Promised Land from their entry into Canaan in the thirteenth century B.C. to the return of the exiles and the restoration of Jewish life in the fifth century B.C. Why the land of *Canaan*? Perhaps because it sat at the crossroads of the world—between Asia, Europe and Africa—where Israel would be God's "light to the nations" (Isa. 42:6).

- **Joshua and the Judges.** Israel's history in Canaan begins with an invasion under Joshua (c. 1250 B.C.), when the Israelites secured footholds in the central hill country of Canaan. The story of Israel taking possession of the land continues for another two hundred years, during the period of the judges. (Israel did not take full control of the land until the reign of David.) The "judges" were charismatic leaders like Deborah, Gideon and Samson whom God raised up to lead Israel when it was attacked by warring neighbors.

27

- **The United and Divided Kingdoms.** The Israelites wanted a king to lead them against their enemies (1 Sam. 8:19–20). Saul was Israel's first king (c. 1020–1000 B.C.). He was followed by David (1000–961), Israel's greatest king. God made a covenant with David, through the prophet Nathan, that a descendant of David would one day rule over a kingdom that would have no end (2 Sam. 7:12–16). In Luke's Gospel, the angel Gabriel tells Mary that her son will inherit "the throne of his ancestor David . . . and of his kingdom there will be no end" (Luke 1:32–33). David was followed by his son Solomon (960–922), who married non-Jewish foreigners for political purposes and "did what was evil in the sight of the Lord" (1 Kings 11:6). After Solomon's death, the united kingdom split in two. The ten northern tribes became the kingdom of Israel; the two southern tribes (Judah and Benjamin) became the kingdom of Judah. Israel was defeated by the Assyrians in 722 B.C. and Judah by the Babylonians in 587 B.C., after which Israel and Judah ceased to exist as separate nations.

- **The Exile in Babylon.** After destroying Jerusalem and Solomon's temple, the Babylonians hauled Israel's leaders off in chains to Babylon. The exile severely tested Israel's faith. The people asked, *What happened?* What happened was foretold by the prophets, who said that God would judge and punish the Israelites if they disobeyed the covenant he made with them at Mount Sinai and if they did not live as a people of "justice and righteousness." In 539 B.C., the Persians defeated the Babylonians. The Persian king, Cyrus, issued an edict that allowed the Jews (those from *Judah*, the remnant tribe) to return to their homeland. The exiles who returned (many did not) found Judah in shambles.

It took men like Nehemiah, who rebuilt the walls around Jerusalem, and Ezra, who reinstituted Jewish religious life, to strengthen the faith of those who returned and took up residence in the Promised Land.

The Voice and Message of the Prophets

During the period of the united and divided kingdoms, Israel became faithless and disobedient. God called prophets to exhort the Israelites to return to the Mosaic Covenant and to prophesy dire consequences if they refused to do so. The word *prophet* comes from a Greek word meaning "one who speaks for another," referring to those called by God to speak his Word ("Thus says the Lord"). The prophets had a special concern for Israel's covenant with God. They came on the scene during the time of the kings; they faded out in postexilic Israel when there were no longer kings.

There are two kinds of prophets in the Old Testament. Prophets such as Nathan, Elijah and Elisha, whose lives and words are woven into the biblical narratives, are called *speaking* or *narrative* prophets. Prophets whose words were written down and collected by their disciples, to be remembered and passed on, are called *writing* or *canonical* prophets. We often think of a prophet as one who speaks about the future, but this was only a minor part—perhaps 10 percent—of the prophets' words to Israel. The prophets' purpose was to address the Israelites in the context of their everyday lives, calling them to return to the Mosaic Covenant.

Elijah is the most important of the precanonical prophets. According to Malachi 3:1 and 4:5, Elijah, who was taken up to heaven in a whirlwind (2 Kings 2:11) in the 800s B.C., will return to announce the coming of the

Messiah. Jesus identifies John the Baptist as the "Elijah figure" sent to proclaim the Messiah (Matt. 17:12–13 and Luke 7:24–28). Amos spoke out against Israel's oppression of the poor and its ritualistic-only worship; he is considered the greatest of the minor prophets. Isaiah is the prophet quoted most often in the New Testament. The book of Isaiah contains prophecies that the New Testament interprets as messianic: the one sent by God will be born of a "virgin" (7:14 and Matt. 1:23); the Spirit will anoint the Messiah "to preach good news to the poor" (61:1 and Luke 4:17–19 NIV); he will come as a suffering servant to bear "the sin of many" (53:12 and Mark 10:45). Jeremiah is the prophet of the new covenant (31:31), which Jesus instituted at the Last Supper.

The Wisdom and Devotional Literature

The remaining five books in the Old Testament comprise the wisdom and devotional literature. Two of them, Psalms and Proverbs, are collections of songs and sayings, without a single author. Job is first in line because its setting is earlier than the other four; Psalms and Proverbs are next, and in this order because David, the patron of psalmic literature, lived before Solomon, the patron of wisdom literature. The other two books are Ecclesiastes, the reflections of an old man who writes that only in God can one find meaning in life, and the Song of Solomon, an allegorical love poem.

- **Psalms.** In contrast to other writings in the Old Testament, the Psalms are Israel's words to God rather than God's words to Israel. It is difficult to date the Psalms, because most do not deal with events in Israel's history to which they can be related; the dates probably range from the united kingdom through the period of the exile. David is given credit for writing seventy-three of the Psalms, but a Psalm *of* David can also mean a Psalm *for* or *dedicated to* David. A unique feature of the Psalms, also seen in the Proverbs, is the parallelism and rhyming of thoughts, with the second line reinforcing the first. The book of Psalms (or Psalter) is the longest book in the Bible, is the book quoted most often in the New Testament, is used in church services for responsive readings and is widely used for personal devotions.

- **Proverbs.** The book of Proverbs contains wonderful advice on how to live in the world, even the twenty-first-century world. There are more than five hundred sayings in all. The book is attributed to Solomon (1:1), but most scholars believe the book of Proverbs is anonymous. The individual proverbs have to do with wisdom, hard work, honesty, self-control, sexual temptation and other matters.

- **Job.** Job is the story of a wise and just man who revered God but lost everything—his flocks, his children, even his health (he suffered from painful, festering sores). The book of Job is a theological discussion of the question of suffering. If God is all-powerful and all-loving, why do the righteous suffer? And why do some suffer more than others? God does not respond to Job's pleas for an answer; instead, he asks Job a question of his own: "Where were you when I laid the foundation of the earth?" (38:4). Job, reflecting on his personal misfortune, says, "Naked I came from my mother's womb . . . the LORD gave, and the LORD has taken away; blessed be the name of the LORD" (1:21).

Judaism Today

Today there are 14 million Jews in the world; 30 percent live in Israel and 40 percent in the United States. *Orthodox* Judaism is the smallest and most legalistic expression of Judaism and the only form of Judaism recognized by the state of Israel. *Reform* Judaism began in Germany in the early 1800s; it sought to reform Judaism to bring it into the mainstream of society. *Conservative* Judaism is a middle course between the legalism of Orthodox Judaism and the liberalism of Reform Judaism.

Judaism and Christianity have many similar beliefs: both believe in a supreme, sovereign God; in the centrality and authority of Scripture; and in an afterlife. The principal differences are as follows. First, Judaism believes that God revealed himself in the Torah, not in a person. Second, Judaism regards God as pure spirit, which precludes his incarnation in a human. Third, Judaism believes that God is one, not triune. Fourth, Judaism has no doctrine of original sin; men and women have inclinations to do good and evil but are not innately sinful. Fifth, Judaism believes that salvation comes through righteous living and faithfulness to the Mosaic Covenant, not through Christ's atoning death.

3

THE WORLD, LIFE AND
MINISTRY OF JESUS

The Old Testament is a story in search of an ending, which comes with the death and resurrection of Jesus of Nazareth. People have managed to do away with many things, but not Jesus. He remains a potent figure—often misunderstood, sometimes disparaged, but always there. We date our calendars with his birth, capture him in art and music and use his teachings as reference points in talking about ethics, morals and justice.

The Intertestamental Period

The period following the return of the exiles from Babylon in 538 B.C. is a period of religious history that remains in the shadows. The walls around Jerusalem were rebuilt under Nehemiah; a modest temple was erected; Jewish religious life was reestablished by Ezra; and the Hebrew Scriptures were gathered together. In 332 B.C., Alexander the Great invaded and conquered Palestine. Alexander loved everything Greek and introduced Greek language, culture and religion wherever he was victorious. In 250 B.C., Jews living in Alexandria (named for Alexander) had to have the Scriptures translated into Greek so that they could be read, resulting in the Septuagint.

Alexander died of a fever at the young age of thirty-three. Because he had no legal heir, his empire was divided among his generals. Seleucus became the ruler of Syria and Palestine. In 167 B.C., the Syrian king Antiochus IV tried to stamp out Judaism, which provoked an uprising led by Judas, whose nickname was *Maccabee* ("the hammer"). The Maccabeans defeated the Syrians in December 164 B.C. and purified the temple, an event that Jews still celebrate as *Hanukkah* ("dedication"). The Jews regained control of their land, but then in 63 B.C. the Romans invaded Palestine to solidify Rome's control of the perimeter of the Mediterranean Sea. This gave them a safe winter land route to bring food from Egypt to Rome. Jesus was born during the reign of Augustus (27 B.C.–A.D. 14), whom historians consider Rome's greatest emperor; Jesus died during the reign of Tiberius (14–37).

The House of Herod

The founder of the house of Herod was Antipater, who came to the aid of Julius Caesar during his Egyptian campaign (48–47 B.C.). Caesar rewarded Antipater with the governorship of Judea and granted the Jews exemption from military service and the freedom to worship their own God. In the year 37 B.C., Marc Antony, the ruler of the eastern half of the Roman Empire, made Antipater's son, Herod, the king of the Jews. Herod was called "the Great" by the Romans (*not* by the Jews) because of his architectural achievements—beautifying Solomon's temple, building the city of Caesarea on the Mediterranean Sea and constructing palace-fortresses like the Antonia Fortress, where Jesus was flogged; Machaerus, where John the Baptist was beheaded; and Masada, near the Dead Sea. Herod ruled Israel from 37 to 4 B.C. In spite of what we may think of him, he must have been an effective administrator, because Rome never removed him.

Upon Herod's death, his empire was divided between three of his sons. Archelaus was an evil, oppressive ruler like his father. In A.D. 6, the Jews sent a delegation to Rome to complain about Archelaus, and he was removed, after which Judea and Samaria were ruled by Rome-appointed governors like Pontius Pilate, who ruled from 26 to 36. Herod Antipas, who had John the Baptist beheaded, ruled Galilee and Perea until he was removed in 39. Philip the *Tetrarch* ("ruler of a fourth") ruled the northeastern territories until his death in 34. Herod Agrippa I, the grandson of Herod the Great, ruled all of Israel from 41 to 44. He was succeeded by his son, Herod Agrippa II, the last Herodian ruler, who died in the year 93.

Jewish Political and Religious Communities

In the first century, the majority of the Jews lived in Judea, in the south. Galilee, where Jesus lived, was heavily Gentile. The Sadducees, who resided in Jerusalem, were the ruling hierarchy. The Pharisees were the "religious" of Israel, along with the scribes. The Essenes lived in semimonastic communities like Qumran (the "monks" of Judaism), whose Dead Sea Scrolls were discovered by a Bedouin shepherd in 1947. The Zealots were the "heirs" of the Maccabees, Israel's freedom fighters.

The most important of these groups were the Sadducees and the Pharisees. The Sadducees were the priestly party and controlled the temple and the Sanhedrin, the ruling council. They regarded Jesus as a dangerous revolutionary who might provoke a riot that would bring down the heavy hand of Rome and were responsible for his death. The Sadducees were linked with the temple; after its destruction in the year 70, they disappeared from the scene.

The Pharisees were lay, fundamentalist Jews and small in number (about six thousand in the first century); they were much admired for their learning and piety. The Pharisees believed that the way to honor God was to keep the law, and they challenged Jesus when they felt he did not do so: for instance, when he ate with sinners, healed the unclean and broke the Sabbath. The Pharisees led the Jewish community after the fall of the temple and determined the books to be received into the Jewish canon.

Outline of Jesus' Life

Jesus was born in 7 or 6 B.C. (see next section). He spent the first thirty-three years of his life in Nazareth, a town of five hundred or so people in lower Galilee. The following is a brief outline of his public ministry.

- In the year 27, John the Baptist, the Elijah-like messenger prophesied by Malachi (3:1 and 4:5), "announces" that Jesus is the one Israel has long been waiting for and baptizes him in the Jordan

River. Jesus receives God's Spirit (Luke 3:21–22) and is led into the wilderness, where he is tested by Satan.

- Following his baptism and testing, Jesus returns to Galilee, proclaiming, "The time has come. . . . The kingdom of God is near. Repent and believe the good news" (Mark 1:15 NIV).

- Jesus calls twelve to be his disciples and begins his ministry, much of which occurs in and around Capernaum, a fishing village and commercial center on the northwest shore of the Sea of Galilee that became his home after he was rejected at Nazareth (Luke 4:28–31). The crowds are amazed at Jesus' teachings and healings but do not recognize him as the hoped-for Messiah.

- Conflicts arise between Jesus and the religious leaders concerning Jesus' association with sinners (tax collectors, lepers, the demon-possessed), his nonobservance of Jewish rituals (washing before meals and fasting) and his breaking the Sabbath law against "work."

- At Caesarea Philippi, Jesus asks his disciples, "Who do you say I am?" Peter answers, "You are the Christ" (Mark 8:29 NIV). Peter gives the right answer, but clearly he and the disciples do not understand that Jesus' mission means suffering and death. This is why they abandon him after his arrest: they think that his mission has failed and that his fate will also be theirs.

- Jesus travels to Jerusalem, where he debates and challenges the religious authorities. He is betrayed by Judas, arrested by the temple guards, tried by the Sanhedrin and Pontius Pilate, beaten and scourged by the soldiers, denied by Peter and crucified between two criminals. He dies, is buried in the tomb of

Joseph of Arimathea—and three days later is raised from the dead to confirm that he was and *is* the very Son of God.

Jesus' Birth

The four Gospels deal with Jesus' public life, from his baptism in the Jordan to his death and resurrection in Jerusalem. Matthew and Luke include birth narratives in their Gospels to add information about Jesus' *origins*; to record that Joseph was from the *line of David*, because the Messiah was to be a "Son of David" (2 Sam. 7:12–16); to show that Jesus' birth in *Bethlehem* fulfilled the prophecy of Micah 5:2; and to begin with Jesus' conception to record that he was *God incarnate* ("God in the flesh") from the very beginning.

Joseph and Mary were the parents of Jesus. Joseph was his "legal" father and Mary his natural mother. We know very little about Joseph; most scholars believe that he died before Jesus began his public ministry. We don't know much about Mary, either, other than that she was young, a virgin, the cousin of Elizabeth and had found favor with God (Luke 1:28). By all accounts she must have been a remarkable woman. There is no way of knowing how old Joseph was when he and Mary became engaged; according to marriage customs in Israel at the time, Mary would have been thirteen or fourteen, much younger than the matronly Mary we are used to seeing in Christian art.

Also, we don't know for certain the year of Jesus' birth. It was most likely two or three years before Herod's death in 4 B.C. because, according to Matthew, Herod gave orders "to kill all the boys in Bethlehem . . . who were two years old and under" (Matt. 2:16 NIV). Nor do we know the day on which Jesus was born. The great celebratory events in the early church were Jesus' death and resurrection (Good Friday and Easter), not his birth. Jesus' supposed birth date—which we celebrate on December 25 as Christmas ("Christ's Mass")—was established in the year 336 by Constantine, the first Christian emperor of the Roman Empire.

Jesus' Baptism, Testing and Disciples

The years before Jesus appeared at the Jordan—the years prior to the year 27—are referred to as Jesus' "hidden years." The event that launches Jesus on his public ministry is his baptism by his cousin John (the two were related through their mothers, according to Luke 1:36). The prophet Malachi had prophesied that Elijah, who was taken to heaven in "a chariot of fire" (2 Kings 2:11), would return to announce the coming of the Lord. Orthodox Jews believe this will still occur. But in the Gospels, John is understood as the Elijah figure who announces Jesus as the long-awaited Messiah, as in Matthew's Gospel, where Jesus tells the disciples that "he [John the Baptist] is the Elijah who was to come" (11:14 NIV).

Following Jesus' baptism, he is tempted or tested by Satan in the Judean wilderness. Inasmuch as Jesus was alone in the wilderness, the account of his testing must have been told to the disciples at a later date, along with other personal material in the Gospels (see Mark 4:34).

The word *disciple* comes from a word meaning "learner." There were disciples in the Old Testament— Isaiah, for instance, had disciples—but the term owes its popularity to the New Testament, where it usually refers to "one of the Twelve." Peter is the spokesperson for the disciples, the one who confesses Jesus to be the Messiah at Caesarea Philippi (Mark 8:29). James and John are also prominent, and together with Peter they

39

comprise the "inner circle" of Jesus' disciples in the Gospels and in Acts. Jesus' disciples came from Galilee, with the possible exception of Judas Iscariot, who most scholars believe came from southern Judea. Jesus chose his disciples from among his many followers—Luke mentions seventy-two (Luke 10:1)—and he commissions the Twelve to be the new "patriarchs" of Israel.

Jesus' Mission

What was Jesus' "mission," that is, what did Jesus come to do? First, he came to reveal God. Jesus said, "Anyone who has seen me has seen the Father" (John 14:9 NIV). Paul writes that Jesus "is the image of the invisible God" (Col. 1:15). The writer of the letter to the Hebrews said that Jesus is "the exact representation" of God (Heb. 1:3 NIV).

Second, he came to inaugurate the kingdom of God, which was both *already* present (in his person) and *not yet* completed ("thy kingdom come").

Third, he came to redeem humankind through his substitutionary death for our sins—for not loving God with our whole heart and mind, for not obeying his commands (1 John 5:3), for not showing love and mercy to our neighbors. The Christian community believes that Jesus' death fulfilled God's plan to send one to bear the sins of the world, as prophesied by Isaiah (53:12), and it regards all of the circumstances surrounding his death, including the betrayal of Judas, as necessary ingredients in this plan.

Jesus' Death

Why was Jesus killed? This is a two-part question. First, why did he go to Jerusalem, knowing that he would be killed there (Mark 10:32–34)? Second, why did the authorities put him to death shortly after he arrived in Jerusalem? As to the first question, Jesus' principal mission was to die a one-time-forever sacrificial death for the sins of the world. If Jesus had died of old age, for instance, he would not have died for our sins.

As to the second question, why did the Sadducees want Jesus killed, and why did Pontius Pilate, knowing that Jesus was innocent (Luke 23:13–15), agree to his crucifixion? The Sadducees were afraid that Jesus would provoke an uprising that would bring a swift, brutal response from Rome—and as Jewish leaders, they would be the first casualties. The reasons for their concern were many: Passover celebrated the deliverance of Israel from foreign rule; it was believed that the Messiah would appear during Passover; Jesus came from Galilee, an area seething with anti-Roman feeling; and Jerusalem was overflowing with Jews who had come to celebrate the Passover. As for Pilate, he was on bad terms with the Jews for erecting emblems of Emperor Tiberius ("graven images") in Jerusalem and for appropriating money from the temple treasury to build an aqueduct. The Jewish leaders told Pilate that "if you let this man go, you are no friend of Caesar" (John 19:12 NIV), implying, perhaps, that they would go to Rome to have him removed, as they had Archelaus.

Jesus' death was by crucifixion, a brutal, cruel, shameful method of execution. Crucifixion was preceded by flogging to weaken the victim's strength, thereby shortening the time it would take him to die. Crosses were hung in public places—Jesus was executed at the Place of the Skull (*Golgotha* in Greek, *Calvary* in Latin)—with a sign telling of the accused's crime as a warning to others. Jesus' sign read "King of the Jews," implying that he claimed to be a king in opposition to the Roman emperor. (The Sanhedrin's charge that Jesus was guilty of blasphemy would not have warranted Roman execution.) The final humiliation came at the end: victims were stripped naked and their bodies left to scavenging birds.

Jesus' Resurrection

The New Testament records twelve accounts of Jesus appearing to his disciples and others after his resurrection. The accounts were written as *fact*, as something that actually occurred, not as theology. They emphasize the element of surprise: no one was expecting what happened on Easter morning, even though Jesus said that he would be raised on the third day (Mark 8:31). And they struggle to describe Jesus' postresurrection body, which was physical—Jesus was able to eat and drink—but could also pass through doors. The Christian writer Frederick Buechner, in his book *The Magnificent Defeat*, said, "Unless something very real took place on that strange, confused morning, there would be no New Testament, no church and no Christianity."

4

THE GOSPEL TESTIMONIES TO JESUS

The word *gospel* derives from the Old English word *god-spel*—"God's [good] story or news." God's *good news* is that "everyone who believes [in Jesus' saving death] shall not perish but have eternal life" (John 3:16, sometimes called the Gospel in a Nutshell). The move from oral to written stories about Jesus—the Gospels—occurred because of the need for an authentic, firsthand account of Jesus by those who knew him (his followers were dying off) and because heretical views of Jesus were beginning to arise.

The Gospels

The Gospels are testimonies to Jesus. They also contain biographical material, but they are not "biographies" in the modern sense, because they cover only 10 percent of Jesus' life and provide no information about his growing-up years in Nazareth or any "personal" material. The concern of the Gospels is not with the *facts* of Jesus' life—so we should not be surprised by occasional differences in the Gospel stories—but with the *meaning* of his life.

- **The Dating of the Gospels.** Most scholars believe that Mark's Gospel was written between 65 and 70, followed by Matthew and Luke in the 80s and John in the 90s. A minority view is that all four Gospels were written before the year 70, because they fail to mention the destruction of the temple by the Romans in that year (see Luke 21:5–6).

- **The Authorship of the Gospels.** It is assumed that because the Gospels are named, we know who wrote them. The Gospels, however, are anonymous; the authors did not add their names to their narratives, as Paul and others did to their letters. This does not mean that we have no idea who wrote them. They were "named" very early. Further, according to British scholar R. T. France, "There is no evidence that any of the Gospels ever existed [without their present names], nor is there any variation in the names of those to whom they are attributed." The names were added in the second century to differentiate the Gospels one from another and for purposes of liturgical reading.

- **The Gospel Audiences.** We read the Gospels as we do other written works. In the first century, however, which had a literacy rate of only 2 or 3 percent, the Gospels were read aloud in house groups rather than privately. To help listeners follow the Gospel narratives, the writers used repetition, especially triads—repeating themes three times—which are found in each of the Gospels.

- **The Structure of the Gospels.** Each of the Gospels has a twofold structure. The first half has to do with Jesus' public ministry: his preaching and teaching, interspersed with healings and miracles to show that Jesus is more than just another teacher. The second half has to do with Jesus' private ministry: preparing the disciples for his coming death in Jerusalem and their apostolic commission—and his resurrection to confirm his divine mission.

Mark: The Foundation Gospel

Mark's Gospel was long neglected because of its alleged incompleteness. Today the opposite is the case, because it is now believed that Mark was the earliest of the four Gospels, thus the original Gospel story, and because Mark served as a source document for Matthew and Luke. (The first three Gospels are called the Synoptic Gospels, the word *synoptic* coming from two Greek words meaning "seeing together," because they have a similar storyline.) Mark's Gospel is action-packed and has a sense of urgency, as if written to Christians hiding in the catacombs and on the run, as seen in his frequent use (some forty times) of words like *at once*, *immediately* and *quickly*.

- **John Mark.** According to church tradition, Mark's Gospel was written from Rome, most likely in the years immediately following Peter's martyrdom in the mid-60s. According to Papias, the second-century bishop of Hierapolis, "Mark became Peter's interpreter and wrote down accurately all that he remembered of the things said and done by the Lord" (the graphic details in Mark's Gospel suggest an eyewitness source). There is no reason to suppose that Mark did not write the Gospel that bears his name, because it is unlikely that it would have been attributed to someone who was neither a disciple nor an apostle unless he was, in fact, the author. According to tradition, then, the author of the first or earliest Gospel was Mark, also called John Mark (Acts 12:12, 25). He was the son of Mary, a widow of some means who lived in Jerusalem (Acts 12:12), whose home may have been the location of the Last Supper. If so, the "young man" in the Garden of Gethsemane (Mark 14:51–52) may be Mark's "secret autograph." (Some think that each Gospel has a secret autograph; others consider such notions little more than silly speculation.) Mark was the cousin of Barnabas; together they accompanied Paul on his first missionary journey (c. 46–48). For some reason, at Perga, Mark left them "to return to Jerusalem" (Acts 13:13). Mark and Paul were later reconciled (2 Tim. 4:11).

- **Structure, Audience and Message.** As mentioned, the Gospels have a two-part structure. The center point or hinge verse in Mark's Gospel is Peter's confession of Jesus as "the Christ" (8:29), following which Jesus tells the disciples that he will "suffer many things and be rejected by the elders . . . and that he must be killed" (8:31 NIV). Mark's readers appear to be Gentiles: there is no Jewish genealogy in his Gospel; there are very few Old Testament references; Jewish words and customs are explained (see 7:3–4); and it is a Gentile, a Roman centurion at the foot of the cross, who declares Jesus to be "the Son of God" (15:39). Many believe that Mark wrote to strengthen the courage and faith of those

suffering persecution as scapegoats for the burning of Rome by Nero in July 64. (Nero burned a
residential section of the city on which he later
built a palace; to counter rumors that he started
the fire, he blamed the Christians.) Mark's message
is that hoping in Jesus is a real hope, just as it was
for Jesus' disciples when he told them that if they
lost their lives "for my sake, and for the sake of the
gospel" they would be saved (8:35).

Matthew: The Jewish Gospel

Matthew was the most popular Gospel in the early
church, for three reasons. First, its author was believed
to have been a disciple, which Mark was not. Second, it is
comprehensive in scope (Matthew has both infancy and
resurrection narratives, which Mark does not). Third,
its organized teachings, like the Sermon on the Mount,
made it ideal for instructing new believers.

If Mark was the first Gospel to be written, why does
Matthew appear first in the canon? Because it was
once believed that Matthew *was* the first Gospel; it is
a more complete narrative (Matthew, like Luke, felt
the need to write a much longer narrative than Mark);
and Matthew portrays Jesus as the one prophesied
about, making his Gospel the best bridge between
the two Testaments. Matthew's masterpiece is Jesus'
Sermon on the Mount.

- **Matthew, the Tax Collector.** The author of the
  second Gospel is "Matthew, the tax collector" (10:3),
  one of Jesus' twelve disciples (in Mark and Luke, he
  is called Levi). Tax collectors were despised because
  they levied taxes on fellow Jews and because they
  allegedly had no principles. (Given the low regard

in which tax collectors were held, it is surprising that Matthew refers to himself as a tax collector; could this be his "secret autograph"?). Some believe that Matthew may have worked for Herod Antipas, collecting custom taxes on merchandise carried from Damascus to Acre, a city on the Mediterranean Sea. As a customs official, Matthew would have known how to write and keep orderly records and could have written down many of Jesus' teachings, which are a central feature of his Gospel. Today there is considerable skepticism regarding the authorship of Matthew's Gospel because it follows Mark's story line and includes 90 percent of Mark's Gospel. (Critics ask, "Why would someone who was with Jesus borrow so heavily from someone who was not?") Some believe that Matthew's Gospel was written by his disciples, which is why they had to rely so heavily on Mark. It is supposed that they took Mark's Gospel, Matthew's collection of Jesus' teachings like the Sermon on the Mount and special materials like Matthew's birth narrative, and wrote an expanded Gospel that they attributed to their teacher or master, Matthew. Today we would call this plagiarism; in the ancient world, where there were no copyright laws or controls, the use of other people's writings was a normal, accepted practice.

- **Structure, Audience and Message.** Matthew follows Mark's story line but adds a different emphasis: Jesus' teachings, which Matthew inserts into Mark's narrative as five *discourses*. The discourses have to do with discipleship (chapters 5–7), mission (10), the kingdom of God (13), community life (18) and the coming judgment (23–25). Matthew's readers appear to be Jewish Christians because Jewish words and customs are not explained (his readers know what he is talking about). Matthew's Jesus is the long-awaited Messiah, which he sets forth in two ways. First, his genealogy from Abraham through David to Joseph shows that Jesus was from the "house" of David. Second, his numerous references to the prophecies of Isaiah, Micah, Hosea, Jeremiah and other prophets show that Jesus "fulfilled" what had been spoken and written about the Messiah in the Hebrew Scriptures.

Luke: The Universal Gospel

Luke's Gospel is the longest book in the New Testament, and Luke-Acts (Luke also wrote the book of Acts) comprises 25 percent of the New Testament. For many people, Luke's Gospel is their favorite "Life of Christ." (Someone once asked the Scottish scholar James Denney to recommend a good book on Jesus. Denney said, "Have you read the one that Luke wrote?") Luke did not know Jesus during his public life; he based his Gospel on the writings and eyewitness accounts of others (see 1:1–4). Luke is careful to name people and to date events as though he is writing history, which he continues in the Acts of the Apostles. His intent, however, is to show God working out his plan of salvation on the plane of history. A special feature of Luke's Gospel is Jesus' parables. Luke tells the most and best loved of Jesus' parables, which he skillfully weaves into his narrative, whereas Matthew and Mark often bunch them together.

- **Luke, the Physician.** From the beginning, tradition has assigned the authorship of the third Gospel to Luke; there must have been compelling reasons to do so, because Luke was not one of Jesus' disciples. It is generally assumed that Luke was a Gentile, though some dispute this because of his knowledge of things Jewish (which could easily have come from Paul). And Luke seems to have been a doctor, given his use of precise medical language and terms and Paul's reference to him as "the doctor" (Col. 4:14). It is believed that Luke met Paul at Troas on Paul's second journey in the early 50s; that he helped Paul start a church at Philippi, which Luke may have pastored; that he later rejoined Paul and accompanied him to Jerusalem at the end of Paul's third journey and then went to Caesarea when Paul was imprisoned there; and that Luke sailed with Paul to Rome at the end of his life. Some think the "we" passages in Acts (16:9–17; 21:1–17; 27:1–28:16) are Luke's secret autograph.

- **Structure, Audience and Message.** Luke also follows Mark's story line, but he is more polished, more literary and more expansive in telling his story. The Irish scholar David Gooding said that Luke's Gospel has two "movements"—Jesus coming from heaven to earth, which begins in the *manger*, and his going from earth to heaven, which ends with his *ascension* (both are unique to Luke). The hinge verse is 9:51. Luke wrote for a Greco-Roman audience, which can be seen in his dedication to Theophilus, his literary style and vocabulary, his frequent use of Greek rather than Hebrew words and his limited reference to Jewish customs. Matthew wrote that Jesus was the promised Messiah; Luke wrote that Jesus was the universal Savior. Luke's genealogy, for instance, goes beyond David and Abraham to Adam: Jesus did not come to save Israel, he came "to seek out and to save [*all* who are] lost" (19:10, emphasis added). Luke's theme or message can be seen in Jesus' homily in the synagogue at Nazareth (4:16–21), in which Jesus announces that he is the one anointed by the Spirit to bring the good news of salvation to the poor, the marginalized and the oppressed.

John: The Spiritual Gospel

John's Gospel stands apart from Matthew, Mark and Luke in terms of structure, style and content; the overlap is only about 10 percent. Some differences can be seen in John's *omissions*: John has no birth narrative, no baptism or temptations, no parables or Beatitudes, no Mount of Transfiguration and no agony in the garden or on the cross. Other differences can be seen in his *additions*: the wedding at Cana, Jesus and Nicodemus, the Samaritan woman at the well, healing the man born blind, washing the disciples' feet and raising Lazarus. A special feature of John's Gospel is Jesus' use of seven "I am" metaphors to describe himself as "the way of salvation." These are passages in which he says "I am the bread of life" (6:35), "the light of the world" (8:12), "the gate" (10:9), "the good shepherd" (10:11), "the resurrection and the life" (11:25–26), "the way, the truth and the life" (14:6) and "the vine" (15:5).

- **John, the Beloved Disciple.** John was the younger brother of James (the Sons of Thunder, Mark 3:17) and most likely the youngest of Jesus' disciples. Many identify him as "the disciple whom [Jesus] loved" (John 19:26), who isn't named, probably out of modesty (John's secret autograph?). Five books in the New Testament bear John's name: the fourth Gospel, the three letters of John (1, 2 and 3 John) and the book of Revelation. With regard to the fourth Gospel, the early church held that John, the son of Zebedee, is "the disciple who testifies

51

to these things and who wrote them down" (21:24 NIV). Today some commentators believe that the fourth Gospel did not come from the "hand" of John but from his followers, referred to as the Johannine Community.

- **Structure, Audience and Message.** As mentioned above, John does not follow Mark's story line, nor is it clear to whom his Gospel is addressed, but he structures his narrative like the other three—a public ministry and a private ministry. The first half (chapters 1–12) has been called the Book of Signs (or Miracles); the second half (13–21) has been called the Book of Glory (Jesus' "hour," his glorification). Many believe that John was writing a testimony to Jesus for the Christian community in Ephesus, where he lived out the final years of his life at the end of the first century. John's message is that Jesus is the one in whom "the Word became flesh" (1:14). William Barclay, the Scottish Bible commentator, said, "This might well be the single greatest verse in the New Testament." Jesus did not come to *bring* the message of eternal life; he *is* the message.

The Gospels: Four Stories, One Jesus

Some say that because the Gospels present different stories and portraits of Jesus, they are fiction. Not at all. When we read multiple biographies of a famous person, we find that the authors tell their stories differently, and each helps us to know the person better than if we had read only one biography. The same is true with the Gospels. The reason they appear different is because each author chose, in shaping his narrative, to emphasize different aspects of the Jesus story for his particular audience. Mark wrote to Christians in Rome who were suffering persecution under Nero. Matthew wrote to Jewish Christians that Jesus was the long-awaited Messiah. Luke wrote to the wider Greco-Roman world that Jesus was the universal Savior. John wrote that Jesus was the one in whom "the Word became flesh." Four testimonies, written from four different perspectives, but all about the same Jesus, who lived and died and rose again.

5

PAUL AND THE OUTWARD MOVEMENT

Jesus' final charge to his disciples in Matthew's Gospel was to take the Good News to "all nations" (28:19), meaning to "all people," and in the book of Acts to "the ends of the earth" (1:8), meaning throughout the Roman Empire.

The Acts of the Apostles

The book of Acts is the story of how Christianity moved from Jerusalem, the center of the Judeo-Christian world, to Rome, the center of the sociopolitical world. It is the second half of Luke's two-volume work on the origins of Christianity. The two books were separated in the second century to combine the four Gospels into one collection and to give Acts a place of its own as the story of the "outward movement" of the Good News.

- **Luke's Authorship.** Luke's authorship of Acts has never been seriously challenged, though some wonder why, if Luke was Paul's traveling companion, he never mentions that Paul wrote letters. The answer may be that Luke chose to emphasize Paul's preaching (there are nine Pauline speeches in Acts), since in antiquity history was often written through the spoken words of the principal characters in the narrative. Others wonder why Luke reintroduces Theophilus at the beginning of Acts and repeats the story of Jesus' ascension (both appear in his Gospel). Perhaps Luke does this because the two books were separate scrolls and this was Luke's way of tying them together.

- **The Story and Structure of Acts.** The book of Acts is the story of the first thirty years of the church—from Jesus' postresurrection appearances and ascension in the year 30 until the arrival of Paul in Rome in the year 60. The first half of the book (chapters 1–12) is the *Petrine* section, the story of Peter and the church in Jerusalem; it ends with the death of Herod Agrippa I in 44. The second half (chapters 13–28) is the *Pauline* section, which begins with the sending out of Paul and Barnabas in the year 46 (13:1–3). This is the story of Paul's missionary work in Philippi, Corinth, Ephesus and other cities in the Roman Empire.

- **Pentecost: The Church's Birthday.** The book of Acts opens with Jesus and the disciples in Jerusalem. In 1:8 (NIV)—a key verse in understanding the structure and message of Acts—Jesus says, "You will receive power when the Holy Spirit comes on you; and you will be my witnesses in Jerusalem, and in all Judea and Samaria, and to the ends of the earth" (in expanding concentric circles). On the first Pentecost after Jesus' death (*Pentecost* comes from a Greek word meaning "fiftieth," to mark the fiftieth day after Passover), the Holy Spirit came upon the disciples and others, who began to speak in "other tongues" (fourteen are mentioned). The Spirit that descended on Jesus at his baptism (Luke 3:22) launched Jesus on his ministry to Israel; the same Spirit came upon his followers at Pentecost, launching them on their ministry to "the ends of the earth."

The Apostle Paul: Ambassador for Christ

The book of Acts introduces us to the apostle Paul, the most important, though not the first or only, of the church's early missionaries. Well before Paul's first journey in the year 46, churches had been established in Damascus, where Ananias and others were active; in Antioch, which had a large Christian community and became Paul's mission base; in Cyprus, Barnabas's native land; in Rome, which had a thriving church years before Paul arrived there; and in Alexandria, the home of Apollos.

- **Saul of Tarsus.** We know quite a bit about Paul from the book of Acts and from his letters (Gal. 1:13–24 and Phil. 3:4–6). He was named for Saul, Israel's first king; Paulus or Paul was his Greco-Roman name. Paul was born in Tarsus in modern-day Turkey, a prosperous port and trade center that was famous for its schools (it was the "Athens of Asia Minor"). His parents were Roman citizens, though it is not known how they obtained their citizenship; Paul says that he inherited his citizenship (Acts 22:27–28). His father was a leather worker and tent maker, as was Paul. He had a sister whose son warned Paul of a plot against him following his arrest in Jerusalem (23:16). When he was old enough, Paul went to Jerusalem to study under Gamaliel (22:3), the most famous rabbinic scholar in the first century. Paul became a strict, zealous Jew who persecuted Christians, whom he thought were undermining Judaism. In the year 33, when Paul was in his late 20s, he met Jesus on the road to Damascus.

- **Paul's Conversion.** The call of Paul is the most dramatic conversion story in the Bible. Paul went to Damascus to hunt for "any there who belonged to the Way" (the way of Jesus). As he approached the city, "a light from heaven flashed around him [and] he heard a voice say to him, 'Saul, Saul, why do you persecute me?'" (Paul was persecuting Jesus' followers.) Paul is told by Ananias that he has been chosen "to carry [Jesus'] name before the Gentiles." The account in Acts 9:1–19 is followed by two parallel accounts, one in Jerusalem following Paul's arrest at the end of his third journey (22:3–21) and another during his imprisonment in Caesarea (26:9–18).

- **Paul's Missionary Journeys.** It is not known how many journeys Paul undertook, but three are well documented in the book of Acts. The first journey team (c. 46–48) included Paul, Barnabas and Mark (for part of the way); they traveled from Antioch to Cyprus (Barnabas's homeland) and then to Galatia. The second journey team (c. 49–53) included Paul, Silas (who replaced Barnabas) and Timothy (who replaced Mark); they went to cities in Asia Minor that Paul had visited on his first journey, and then they traveled to Europe, ending in Corinth, where Paul stayed for eighteen months. (It was on this journey that Luke met Paul.) On the third journey (c. 54–58), Paul and his same team revisited churches they had established in Asia Minor and Europe and then settled in Ephesus, where Paul stayed for two years.

- **Paul's Writings.** Paul's writings follow the Greco-Roman style, with his name at the beginning, followed by a formal greeting; then the body of the letter, which included both doctrinal teachings and ethical instructions; and some final greetings at the end. Paul's letters were written over a period of some fifteen years—from 1 Thessalonians in 50–51 to the Pastoral Letters in the 60s. His letters were usually dictated (see Rom. 16:22); were carefully written, though some may have been edited and combined, as with the Corinthian correspondence; were more numerous than those in the New Testament (the letters referred to in 1 Cor. 5:9; 2 Cor. 2:4; and Col. 4:16 have never been found); and were both communal (written to churches) and personal (like the letters to Timothy). Some believe that Luke assembled Paul's correspondence from copies Paul made of his letters; others believe the letters were gathered together by Onesimus (the slave mentioned in Paul's letter to Philemon), who later became the bishop of Ephesus.

- **Paul's Theology.** Paul grew up believing that the Torah was God's ultimate revelation—then Jesus appeared to him on the road to Damascus, and everything changed. Paul came to understand that while Jewish law made one aware of sin, it had no *power* over sin. Only by faith, only by believing in Jesus, the one sent to redeem us from our sins, can we be *justified*—"justification by faith," Paul's doctrinal center—and rightly related to God. The bottom line of Paul's theology is the cross: "We preach Christ crucified: a stumbling block to Jews and foolishness to Gentiles" (1 Cor. 1:23 NIV).

• **Paul: The Ideal Man.** Paul was the ideal man in the ideal place at the ideal time to launch God's mission to the Gentiles: he was a *Pharisaic Jew* who was firmly grounded in the Hebrew Scriptures; a *non-Palestinian Jew* who was able to translate the gospel into the language and thought forms of the Greco-Roman world; a *Roman citizen* who was protected by his rights of citizenship; and a *religious zealot*, first on behalf of Judaism, and then Christianity. During his dozen years on the mission field (46–58), the apostle Paul established churches in several northern Mediterranean cities of the Roman Empire.

Galatians: The Epistle of Christian Freedom

Galatians has been called the Magna Carta of Christian liberty (from Jewish legalism). After Paul left Galatia, some *Judaizers*—hard-line Jewish Christians—arrived. They told the Galatians that Paul's teaching that we are saved by grace through faith was not enough; it needed to be more firmly grounded in Judaism. Though the Judaizers were a headache, they forced Paul to articulate the principal distinguishing differences between Christianity and Judaism, those that made Christianity separate and distinct from, rather than an extension of, Judaism. Paul said that a person is not justified by works of the law (Jewish rules, rituals and customs) but through faith in Jesus Christ. If justification comes through the law, Paul said, "then Christ died for nothing" (2:15–21). The letter to the Galatians contains Paul's nine fruits of the Spirit, which should be seen in the lives of those who call themselves

Christian: love, joy, peace, patience, kindness, goodness, faithfulness, gentleness and self-control (5:22–23).

Romans: Paul's Magnum Opus

Paul's letter to the church in Rome is considered to be his most important writing: the culmination of his thinking after many years on the mission field; the most systematic statement of his understanding of the gospel; and his last will and testament to the church. No one knows who founded the church in Rome; some think it may have been travelers from Rome who were in Jerusalem on the first Pentecost (see Acts 2:10). The Roman church was a large church; Nero could not have blamed the Christians for burning Rome if they had been a small, insignificant minority.

Romans 1:16–17 has been called the Gospel According to Saint Paul. Paul writes that the gospel "is the power of God for salvation to everyone who has faith [in Jesus Christ]." Paul goes on to say that God has revealed himself in creation and to Israel, but "all have sinned" (3:23). The bad news is that "the wages of sin [the payment for sin] is death"; the good news is that God has sent one to redeem us from our sins, namely, "Christ Jesus our Lord" (6:23). Some call Romans 12:1–15:13 Paul's Sermon on the Mount. He begins by telling the Romans to offer themselves "as *living* sacrifices . . . to God [in contrast to Israel's dead animal sacrifices] . . . [and to] be *transformed* by the renewing [of their] mind" (12:1–2 NIV, emphasis added). Paul goes on to write that Christians are to love one another with mutual affection; contribute to the needs of the saints; extend hospitality to strangers; welcome those who are weak in faith; and never put a stumbling block in the way of another.

The Corinthian Correspondence

Paul and his team visited Corinth on their second journey and stayed for eighteen months. First Corinthians
is an answer to a number of problems that surfaced in
the Corinthian church after Paul left; it shows how the
early church struggled to be Christian in a pagan environment. Those who say, "I wish we could get back to the
simplicity of the early church," should read Paul's first
letter to the Corinthians. In it Paul addresses a number
of issues that were brought to him in person (1:11) and
in writing (7:1). Space does not allow for their discussion, but they involve problems the church is struggling
with even today: cliques and factions, sexual immorality,
marriage and divorce, sensitivity toward new believers,
propriety in worship and the proper exercise of spiritual
gifts. Chapter 15 is Paul's great chapter on the resurrection: he mentions those to whom Jesus appeared after his
resurrection, the future resurrection of all who "belong"
to Christ and the nature of our to-be-resurrected bodies.
Paul's second letter to the Corinthians is the most auto-
biographical of his letters. In it he defends his ministry
against the "super apostles"; he also talks about his "thorn
in the flesh" (12:7). The letter ends with the popular,
widely used benediction, "May the grace of the Lord
Jesus Christ, and the love of God, and the fellowship of
the Holy Spirit be with you all" (13:14 NIV).

Paul's Other Letters

Most scholars believe that First Thessalonians was
Paul's first letter, which would make it the first New
Testament "book" to be written. This letter and Second
Thessalonians address questions that arose in Thessa-
lonica after Jews there forced Paul to leave (Acts 17).

Their questions had to do with Jesus' return, specifically what happens to those who die before he returns (1 Thess. 4:13–18).

Paul wrote four letters while he was in prison, which are called the Prison Epistles. Philippians is Paul's letter of great joy to his favorite church. Colossians is a letter written to a church that Paul had neither founded nor visited concerning certain heresies that had arisen in the church in Colossae. Philemon is a personal letter to a member of the Colossian church about his runaway slave, Onesimus. Ephesians is the most important of the Prison Epistles. It contains a theme central to Protestant theology: we are saved by grace through faith, not by works (2:8–10).

The remaining three Pauline letters are called the Pastoral Letters. They contain instructions from the pastor Paul to two young pastors, Timothy and Titus, to maintain orthodoxy, to rebuke false teachers and to be models of Christian conduct. Paul also gives characteristics to look for in choosing church leaders (1 Tim. 3:1–13).

The Letter to the Hebrews and the Seven General Letters

There are eight letters that follow Paul's letters. Hebrews is first in line because it is the longest non-Pauline letter. The letter establishes the all-sufficiency of Jesus' sacrifice for our sins (see 10:1–18). Chapter 11 has been called the Faith Hall of Fame.

The seven short letters between Hebrews and Revelation are called the General Letters; they are known by the names of their authors rather than their addressees. The most important are James, 1 Peter and 1 John. James is the famous *faith plus works* epistle of the New Testament. James writes that "faith without deeds is dead" (2:26 NIV). First Peter is the Epistle of Courage. Peter tells his readers to accept their suffering with cheer-fulness, looking to Jesus and following "in his steps" (2:21). First John is written against those who denied Jesus' true humanity. John starts his letter by saying, "We have heard . . . we have seen . . . and touched with our hands" the risen Christ (1:1).

The Book of Revelation

It goes without saying that the book of Revelation is one of the most difficult books in the Bible, and also one of the most controversial. One reason is its use of symbolic language (numbers, colors, strange phenom-ena). We should remember that the author's symbols would have been understood by those to whom he was writing, much as the number thirteen would be today. For instance, *horns* (of animals) were a symbol of power, and *seven* symbolized fullness or completeness; thus seven horns meant all-powerful and seven eyes meant all-seeing. The message of apocalyptic literature like Revelation is that God will save his people, as he did when Pharaoh was oppressing the Israelites in Egypt. Until God intervenes, however, things will likely get even worse. But God will prevail and will reward those who have been steadfast and faithful.

The book of Revelation has two parts. First, John is told to write what is revealed to him concerning seven churches (meaning, perhaps, the "whole church") in present-day Turkey, whose members were guilty of compromise and apostasy (abandoning their beliefs). Second, John is shown visions of plagues, famine, wars and death, each described in vivid language, and is told that there will be a final battle—the Battle of Armaged-don—following which Satan will be bound and there will be "a new heaven and a new earth" (21:1).

Why Didn't the Jews Accept Jesus as the Messiah?

The book of Acts and Paul's letters tell the story of the outward movement of the good news. Although many Jews believed that Jesus was the promised Messiah, as reported in Acts 2:41, 2:47 and 4:4, the overwhelming majority, both in Palestine and in the cities Paul visited on his journeys, did not. Why not? First, the Jews believed that the Messiah would be a royal figure from Jerusalem, the City of David, not a peasant from an insignificant village in Galilee. Second, they believed that the Messiah would embody the highest purity of Judaism, not eat with tax collectors, heal the unclean and break the Sabbath. Third, Jews, at least zealot Jews, were waiting for a military Messiah like David who would lead Israel in the overthrow of Rome, not someone who said, "Love your enemies and pray for those who persecute you" (Matt. 5:44). Fourth, the Jews did not understand that the Messiah would bear the sins of Israel, as prophesied by Isaiah (chapter 53), or that he would be crucified, because one hanged on a tree (on a cross) was under God's curse (Deut. 21:23). Fifth, the Jews did not believe that the Messiah would be raised from the dead in the middle of time; they believed that he would be raised, along with everyone else, at the end of time.

God's plan is to bring salvation to the whole world. The centerpiece of this plan is Jesus Christ, who died a sacrificial death for the sins of the world and was raised from the dead to confirm his mission. In his first letter to the Corinthians, Paul calls Jesus' death "a stumbling block to Jews," who were looking for a king, not a suffering servant, and "foolishness to Gentiles," who wondered how one crucified as a common criminal could be the world's Savior (1 Cor. 1:23).

6

A BRIEF HISTORY
OF CHRISTIANITY

During the first thousand years of the Common Era, the Christian church was one church. In the year 1054, there was a schism or separation, which divided the church into Roman Catholic and Eastern Orthodox. Five centuries later, a German monk named Martin Luther posted his famous "Ninety-five Theses" on the door of the Castle Church in Wittenberg, igniting the Protestant Reformation and splitting the Western church into Catholic and Protestant. In the years following the Reformation, first Catholic and then Protestant missionaries took the gospel to India, sub-Saharan Africa, the New World and the Far East.

The Patristic Period

The four centuries following the death and resurrection of Jesus are called the Patristic Period—the period of the early church fathers—which ended in the fifth century when the Visigoths invaded and sacked Rome. This is the period of the formation of the church by the apostles and their successors; the collection of Christian writings and the church's agreement on the books to be included in the New Testament canon; the "conversion" of Emperor Constantine in 312 and the establishment of Christianity as the official religion of the Roman Empire in 380; and the councils of Nicea (325), Constantinople (381) and Chalcedon (451), which hammered out the basic beliefs of Christianity.

The most important church father was Augustine (354–430), who grew up in North Africa and was converted in a garden in Milan in the year 386 while reading a passage from Paul's letter to the Romans (13:13–14). In 387, Augustine became the bishop of Hippo, the modern city of Annaba in Algeria. Augustine's writings shaped the theology of the church regarding the doctrine of *original sin*, based on Paul's letter to the Romans (5:12–14); God's free, unmerited *gift of grace*, which had come to Augustine, as it had to Paul; the equality of the "persons" in the *Trinity*; and the church as the *channel* of God's grace. Next to Paul, Augustine did more to shape the thinking and theology of the church than any other person.

The Middle Ages

The Roman Empire lasted for more than twelve hundred years—from the founding of Rome in 753 B.C. to its fall in A.D. 476. During the first centuries of the Christian or Common Era, Rome ruled all the lands bordering on the Mediterranean Sea. At the height of Rome's power, under Emperor Trajan (who reigned from 98 to 117), the empire's borders embraced some 2 million miles and had an estimated population of 50 million people, only a small minority of whom, however, were Roman citizens. In the year 410, the Visigoths entered and sacked the city of Rome and then left. Rome finally fell in the year 476. The fall of Rome was the fall of the Western Empire; the Eastern or Byzantine Empire, with its capital at Constantinople (the "City of Constantine"), continued for another thousand years, falling to the Ottoman Turks in 1453. The reasons for the fall of Rome include weak leadership, moral decay and Rome's inability to finance and maintain an army sufficient to protect itself from aggressive, warring neighbors. Some call the thousand or so years after the fall of Rome the Dark Ages, but a great deal was going on, especially in the church.

- **Rome and the Papacy.** The church in Rome was the most important church in Christendom: it was situated in the ancient capital of the empire; it had the largest congregation of Christians; and its roots went back to Peter and Paul, whose martyred remains were buried there. (It is said that Peter's bones lie beneath the altar in Saint Peter's Basilica.) When Rome fell, the Roman church became the dominant institution in Europe. It claimed that Peter, the chief of the apostles (Matt. 16:18), had passed on to subsequent bishops of Rome his authority as Christ's vicar or representative on earth, which gave the bishop of Rome authority over all other bishops. In the fifth century, the bishop of Rome began to be called the *pope*, from the Latin *papa*, meaning "father."

69

- **The Catholic-Orthodox Schism.** The schism (or division) between the Western church in Rome and the Eastern church in Constantinople occurred in 1054. The Western and Eastern churches were separated by *distance* (one thousand miles), by *language* (the West spoke Latin and the East spoke Greek) and by *authorities* (the West followed the pope and the East followed the ecumenical, churchwide councils). In addition, the Eastern church venerated icons—paintings of Jesus, Mary and the saints that were used for teaching and devotions—which the West viewed as "graven images"; it used unleavened bread for the Eucharist; and its clergy could marry (before ordination but not after). In the year 1054, Pope Leo IX excommunicated Cerularius, the patriarch of Constantinople, for overstepping his authority. Cerularius returned the favor, and the church split into *Roman Catholic*, meaning allegiance to Rome and the church as catholic or universal, and *Orthodox*, meaning true or correct belief.

- **The Crusades** (1095–1291). The Crusades were a series of major and minor military campaigns to expel the Muslims from the Holy Land, which had been under Muslim control since 638. Pope Urban II launched the first crusade in 1095, promising a total pardon for past sins to those who responded. The first crusade was the most successful, recapturing Jerusalem in 1099, only to lose it again in 1187. The other crusades were not successful—in fact, many ended in dishonor as the crusaders turned their attention from recapturing the holy places of Christendom to pillaging and rape.

- **Thomas Aquinas** (1225–1274). Thomas Aquinas grew up in Aquino, near Naples, Italy. A brilliant, deeply religious man, Aquinas entered the Dominican order in 1244, to the great displeasure of his noble family, and became the greatest philosopher and theologian of the Catholic Church. (In 1880, Pope Leo XIII made Aquinas the patron saint of all Catholic schools and universities.) Aquinas attempted to construct a synthesis between biblical theology (faith) and natural theology (reason), believing that it was possible, through the use of reason, to come to the knowledge of God. One example was his five "proofs" of the existence of God: movement, causation, perfection, contingency and design.

- **Monasticism.** One response to the church's institutionalization was monasticism, a way of showing one's devotion to Jesus by living a life of prayer, study, meditation, fasting and also celibacy, which the Second Lateran Council in 1139 declared to be the rule or norm for priests and others called to the religious life. Communal monasticism began in Egypt in the 300s. It blossomed in the West under Benedict of Nursia (Italy), the "father" of Western monasticism, whose rules—The Rule of Saint Benedict—regarding community life, prayer, study and daily manual labor set the pattern for monks to this day. (*Monk* comes from the Latin *monachos*, meaning "one who lives alone.")

The Protestant Reformation

The Reformation—the effort to "reform" the church—split the Western church into Catholic and Protestant. The reformers "protested" against many aspects of the church: the *papal system*, which concentrated power in the pope and the *curia* (the agencies used to administer the church); the *immorality* and *corruption* of the clergy, some of whom used their positions for personal gain; the church's *oppression*, the most violent form being the Spanish Inquisition; and abuses relating to the church's sale of *indulgences* to finance the building of Saint Peter's Basilica in Rome. (Indulgences were written "pardons" thought to shorten one's time in purgatory—in Catholicism, the place where souls are purified of unforgiven venial sins so they may enter heaven.) Another factor in the Reformation was a growth in nationalism that challenged the dominance of Rome; this challenge was led by princes in Germany and elsewhere in Europe and monarchs such as Henry VIII of England.

- **Martin Luther** (1483–1546). The event that formally ignited the Reformation occurred when Martin Luther, a professor of theology at the University of Wittenberg, posted his famous *Ninety-five Theses Against Indulgences* on the door of the Castle Church at Wittenberg, Germany, on October 31, 1517. Luther's theses, which were printed and circulated throughout Germany, were an invitation to the church to discuss abuses relating to the "sale" of indulgences. Luther believed in the forgiveness of sins by and through Christ, which required no payments to the church. Luther was asked to renounce his views. He refused and was charged with heresy and excommunicated (denied the church's sacraments). Luther's teachings stressed the sole sufficiency of God's *grace*; *faith* as the only means for its reception; *Scripture* as the sole norm for faith and life; and Christ as the world's only *Savior*—summarized as "grace alone, faith alone, the Word alone, and Christ alone."

- **John Calvin** (1509–1564). The other giant figure of the Reformation was the Frenchman John Calvin, a second-generation reformer who was twenty-five years Luther's junior. Calvin lived in French-speaking Geneva. His great contribution to the Reformation was the *Institutes of the Christian Religion*, a systematic statement of Reformation theology. Calvin wrote, revised and expanded the *Institutes* four times over the years 1536–1559 (the first version was written when Calvin was only twenty-seven years old). During and after Calvin's lifetime, Geneva became the center of the non-Germanic Protestant world.

- **Protestant-Catholic Differences.** Some differences between Reformation thought and Roman Catholicism were as follows. First, Reformation theology was based on the Bible and the Bible alone (*sola Scriptura*); Catholic theology gave equal weight to the teachings of the church fathers.

    Second, the Reformers translated the Bible into the vernacular so that it could be read by the people; the Catholic Bible was Latin only and the church was its sole interpreter.

    Third, the Reformers taught that salvation was "by grace . . . through faith" (Eph. 2:8); the Catholic Church held itself to be the exclusive channel by which salvation was made available, through the sacraments, to the people.

    Fourth, the Reformers believed in the "priesthood of all believers," which eliminated divisions between the clergy and the laity.

    Fifth, the Reformers saw no scriptural basis for a priest to "dispense" God's grace; they emphasized, instead, each person's direct access to God through Jesus (1 Tim. 2:5).

- **The Fourfold Reformation.** The Protestant Reformation was not a *single* reformation but *several* reformations, which expressed themselves in different forms. *Lutheranism* was based on the teachings of Martin Luther. *Calvinism*, which was much more "Protestant" than Lutheranism, was based on the teachings of John Calvin, which differed from those of Luther regarding church polity, the Lord's Supper and other matters. The *English Reformation* was more political than theological, at least at the outset. Henry VIII (who reigned from 1509 to 1547) wanted a male heir to his throne. His wife, Catherine of Aragon, was in her forties, and the prospects for a son were not promising, so in 1533 he divorced her. This was not allowed under Catholic canon law, and Henry was excommunicated. (Catherine's nephew, Charles V, was the Holy Roman Emperor and an ally of the pope). In 1534, the British Parliament made the king the head of the Church of England.

  The *Radical Reformation* went beyond Luther and Calvin. Its leaders wanted a simple, less liturgical form of worship and a congregational form of government. The Radical Reformers included the *Puritans*, who wanted to "purify" the Church of England of its Romanism; the *Separatists*, who separated from the Church of England and came to America, where they founded Congregational churches; the *Baptists*, who baptized by immersion after a believer's public profession of faith; the Society of Friends, or *Quakers*, who declared that all should "quake" before the Word of God; and the *Methodists*, who believed that all should observe the "method of life" laid down in the Bible.

- **The Council of Trent.** When the Reformation began to take root and spread, the Catholic Church was forced to meet it head-on and called the Council of Trent (in northern Italy), which met in three long sessions over the years 1545 to 1563. Trent reaffirmed Catholic doctrines challenged by the Reformers, increased papal authority over the church and condemned and abolished certain abuses, including the sale of indulgences.

Christian Missions

There have been four important periods of mission activity in the history of the church. The first occurred during the years between the death of Jesus and the conversion of Constantine (312), when Christianity was transformed from a small Palestinian sect into a community of believers representing perhaps 10 percent of the inhabitants of the Roman Empire. The second took place in the first half of the Middle Ages with the Christianization of Europe. The third took place in the 1500s with the discovery of the Americas and the Far East. The fourth took place in the 1800s with missions into the interiors of India, Africa and China. The driving force behind the overseas expansion of Christianity was the desire for silk, spices and other items of trade and for gold and silver.

In the years following the Reformation, Catholicism won more converts outside Europe than it lost to Protestantism within Europe. There were two reasons for the Catholic Church's success: first, the great naval powers, Spain and Portugal, were Catholic; second, the church had a trained "army" of missionaries—Jesuits, Dominicans and others—who accompanied sea captains like Columbus on their overseas voyages.

The Catholic missionary movement began with Francis Xavier (1506–1552), a Spanish Jesuit who took the gospel to Goa, India, in the 1540s. The Protestant missionary movement began with William Carey (1761–1834), an English Baptist who took the gospel to Calcutta, India, in the early 1800s, and J. Hudson Taylor (1832–1905), who penetrated the interior of China in the late 1800s. At the end of the twentieth century, there were an estimated 2 billion Christians (33 percent of the world's population). According to the *Christian World Encyclopedia* (2001), Christians are divided roughly 50-40-10 percent between Catholic, Protestant and Eastern Orthodox, respectively.

Pentecostalism

The most significant development in Christianity in the last hundred years has been Pentecostalism, which originated in the United States in the early 1900s. According to church demographer David Barrett, Pentecostals and charismatics combined, in January 2000, numbered 524 million (25 percent of Christians worldwide). One reason for Pentecostalism's exploding growth is the desire of many for a more experiential faith. Pentecostals (called such because the first sign of the Spirit came on the first Pentecost after Jesus' death) believe that speaking in *tongues* (other languages) is a sign of being "baptized in the Spirit." Closely aligned with the Pentecostals are the *charismatics*, from a Greek word meaning "gifts," who belong to mainline and other churches. They also emphasize the gifts of the Spirit, but are not insistent on speaking in tongues as the only evidence of the Spirit.

7

CHRISTIAN DOCTRINES AND BELIEFS

What are the bottom-line, nonnegotiable beliefs of Christianity? The early church addressed this issue and came up with creeds and confessions like the Apostles' and Nicene creeds. The better we understand and can articulate our Christian beliefs, which the creeds help us to do, the more confident we will be in sharing our faith.

God Our Father: All-mighty and All-loving

Christian theology has to do first of all with God. The Christian confession is a statement of faith—"I *believe* in God the Father"—rather than something that can be empirically proven.

- **The Knowledge of God.** The knowledge of God comes to us in four ways. First, God is made known in *creation*. Reasoning from what we observe of the world around us, we arrive at a Creator of the universe. Something cannot come from nothing; there must have been a first cause. Second, God is made known in *providence*—his "provide-ence" for his people, as when he heard the Israelites' cries in Egypt and came to their rescue. Third, God is made known in *human conscience*, the aspect of the human psyche that distinguishes right from wrong and urges us to do the right and not the wrong. Fourth, and most important, God is made known in *Jesus*, the "image of the invisible God" (Col. 1:15), the one in whom, Søren Kierkegaard said, "the infinite became finite."

- **The Attributes of God.** People want clarity in thinking about God. How do we visualize God, who is spirit (John 4:24)? One way is to think of God in anthropomorphic (human) terms, as in Michelangelo's painting of God and Adam on the ceiling of the Sistine Chapel in Rome. Another is to reflect on God's attributes and characteristics. God is *eternal*: everything began with God; there was no time when God "was not"; God is "from everlasting to everlasting" (Ps. 90:2). God is *almighty*: he is omnipotent, able to do "whatever pleases him" (Ps. 135:6 NIV); he is omnipresent, everywhere present at one and the same time (Ps. 139:7–12); he is omniscient, having complete and perfect knowledge of things past, present and future (Heb. 4:13). God is the *Creator*: he created the universe and life in all its varied forms (Gen. 1:1–26), and he created out of nothing rather than forming what already was; before God created, there was nothing except God. God is *transcendent* and *immanent*: he is both

78

beyond all that is, as in his creation of the universe, and present and active, as in the exodus, when he freed the Israelites from Egypt, and in Jesus of Nazareth. God is *personal*: he is a person—a person who wants to have a relationship with us—not an object or an it. Three of God's personal attributes are love, mercy and compassion.

- **The Trinity of God.** There are two great mysteries in Christianity. One is the *incarnation*—the doctrine that God entered human history in the person of Jesus of Nazareth to die a sacrificial death for our sins. The other is the *Trinity*—the doctrine that God comes to us in three "persons": as God the *Father*, who created the heavens and the earth and life in all its fullness and variety; as God the *Son*, who came to reveal the invisible God and to rightly relate us to God and to one another; and as God the *Spirit*, who calls us to faith and regenerates and sanctifies us. The Trinity is like a rainbow: each color is distinct and separate from the others, but all are part of the same "bow."

Sin: The Human Predicament

Man and woman were the crown of God's creation, but the first "parents" of the human race fell into sin. And because the human race is interconnected—Augustine said that we are all part of the same "lump"—we as their "children" are fallen as well.

- **The Doctrine of Sin.** Sin is a theological concept: it is disobedience to the divine law and will of God. One Greek word for sin is *hamartia*, which means "missing the mark." We miss the mark when we step over the line and also when we don't step up to the line. What is the mark or line? In a word, it is *love*. We sin when we do not love God with our whole heart, when we disobey his will and commands (1 John 5:3) and when we do not show love and compassion to others. The doctrine of sin has two aspects. First, our inborn sinfulness gives rise to sinful acts, sometimes called "actual sins" or "daily sins." We are not sinful because we sin; rather, we sin because we are sinful. Second, Christ died to redeem us from our sins so that we would not "perish" in our sins.

- **Original Sin.** The origin of sin and evil is second only to the origin of life as the greatest of all enigmas. Where did sin come from? How is it that human beings become evil people? Most religions have a doctrine of sin. Some believe that sin comes from uncontrollable cravings; others believe that we are born neutral and are pushed one way or the other by good and evil forces. Christianity believes that sin is part of the human condition and has been since the dawn of history. Today we see the reality of sin and evil everywhere: terrorism and violence, the use of drugs and other harmful substances, spousal and child abuse, corruption in government and business, racial conflicts and ethnic cleansings. The English writer G. K. Chesterton, in his spiritual autobiography *Orthodoxy*, said that sin is one Christian doctrine that no one can dispute—all you have to do is read the morning newspaper. Today we might say all you have to do is watch the evening news on television.

  How are we to understand the story of Adam and Eve? Some believe that stories must be historical to be true and read Genesis 3 as the account of sin entering the world through the disobedience of Adam and Eve, which Paul elaborates on in Romans

5:12–14. Others believe that stories themselves contain truths, as with Jesus' parables (there was no *actual* Good Samaritan), and read the "fall" of Adam and Eve as a story that conveys an indisputable truth: men and women are sinful, fallen creatures and have been since the beginning of time. The real issue, though, is not how sin entered the human race but sin's deadly consequences—not how we got into this mess, but how we get out. The Christian answer is Jesus Christ, who gave his life as a "ransom" (Mark 10:45) for the sins of those who put their faith and trust in him.

Jesus Christ: Lord and Savior

The fundamental question asked by every religious person is the question of the Philippian jailer in the book of Acts: "What must I do to be saved [rightly related to God]?" (16:30). Paul's answer to the jailer is, "Believe on the Lord Jesus, and you will be saved" (16:31).

- **Jesus' Virgin Birth.** The virginal conception of Jesus in Mary's womb by the power of the Holy Spirit is set forth in the Matthean and Lukan birth narratives. They do not *prove* Jesus' virginal conception; rather, they *announce* that Jesus was God incarnate from the very beginning. Luke, who tells us that he investigated "everything carefully" (Luke 1:3), may have learned about Jesus' conception and birth from Mary while Luke was in Caesarea when Paul was imprisoned there in the late 50s (Mary is believed to have lived into the 60s). Today the virgin birth is a stumbling block for many—even many Christians. British theologian Keith Ward said the strongest argument for the veracity of the

81

birth narratives is that it is hard to see why they would have been invented when their claim—that a child born out of wedlock was the genetic, messianic descendant of King David—would have been so offensive to Jewish ears.

- **Jesus' Saving Death.** The twentieth-century British novelist Dorothy Sayers said no one would deny that there is a wide and deep cleavage in Christendom, "but it does not run between Catholics and Protestants; it runs between those who believe that salvation is of God and those who believe that salvation is of man." Christianity believes that we are saved "by grace . . . through faith" (Eph. 2:8). The first part of the equation is God's gift of *grace* (Jesus' death "for us"), which is totally free. There is nothing that we can do to earn our salvation, nothing that will oblige God to save us. The second part of the equation is accepting, *through faith,* Jesus' death on our behalf. (Karl Barth, the twentieth century's most influential theologian, said that the most important word in the New Testament is the Greek word *huper,* which means "on behalf of," referring to Jesus' substitutionary death for our sins.) Theologians refer to Jesus' on-our-behalf death as the *atonement.* To understand atonement, we have to go back to ancient Israel, where priests sacrificed animals to cover the sins of the people (Leviticus 1–7). The prophet Isaiah said that one is coming who will bear the sins of the people in his own body (Isa. 53:12); Jesus told his disciples that this prophecy "must be fulfilled in me" (Luke 22:37). We accept God's gift of saving grace by believing, trusting and confessing that Jesus' death was, is and will be sufficient for salvation and by living under his lordship.

- **Jesus' Bodily Resurrection.** There were many messianic movements before and after Jesus; they all collapsed with the deaths of their founders. Why did the "Jesus movement" survive—not only survive, but *flourish*? In a word, it was Jesus' resurrection. What is the evidence for Jesus' resurrection? First, the *empty tomb*. If the Jews had produced Jesus' body, they would have put an end to his followers' claim that he had risen from the dead. Second, the *testimony to Jesus' resurrection*. The New Testament contains twelve accounts of the risen Christ. No one would have taken the time or gone to the expense of writing about an executed Jewish peasant from rural Galilee if he had remained in the grave. Third, the *witness of the disciples*, who fled when Jesus was arrested but after Pentecost came out of hiding to preach his resurrection. Many were martyred for doing so—and no one willingly puts his or her life on the line for a lie. Fourth, the discovery of the empty tomb by *the women*. Women were not considered credible witnesses in the first century. If the Gospel writers had fabricated their stories, they would have had men, not women, as the first witnesses.

The Holy Spirit: The Perfecter of Our Faith

The Holy Spirit—or Holy Ghost, from the Old English word *gast*, meaning "spirit"—is the third person of the Trinity. The Spirit is a *person*, not some vague "it" or "force." As to the work of the Spirit, one function is to grant specific *gifts* to believers, some twenty of which are listed in the New Testament (see 1 Cor. 12:8–11; Rom. 12:6–8). Two other works are the *regeneration* of believers, enabling them to be born "again" or "anew" or "from above" (John 3:3–8), and *sanctification*, the continuing work of the Spirit that enables believers to grow in holiness. How does one receive the Holy Spirit? Most sacramental (liturgical) denominations believe that one receives the Spirit at baptism; others believe that a necessary precedent to receiving the Spirit is a public profession of one's faith in Jesus as Lord and Savior.

The Church: Marks and Sacraments

The Nicene Creed confesses four marks of the church, namely, that it is *one* (one body under the lordship of Christ), *holy* (set apart for Christian ministry), *catholic* (universal) and *apostolic* (called to proclaim Jesus). Sacramental churches believe that sacraments are "channels" of grace. The Belgian Dominican theologian Edward Schillebeeckx said, "Just as we encounter God in the tangible Jesus, so we encounter Jesus in the tangible sacraments." The church has long recognized the two sacraments instituted by Jesus, called the "Gospel Sacraments": *Baptism* (Matt. 28:19) and *Eucharist* ("thanksgiving"), also called *Communion* ("common union") and the *Lord's Supper* (Luke 22:19). In addition, Catholic and Orthodox churches recognize as sacraments *Confirmation*, the confirming of vows made by one's parents and sponsors at baptism; *Penance* or *Reconciliation*, previously called *Confession*, the forgiveness of postbaptismal sins; *Matrimony*, the covenanting together of a man and woman in the sight of God; *Ordination* or *Holy Orders*, the consecration of those set apart for Christian ministry; and *Anointing the Sick*, the sacrament of healing.

The End Times

Where is history headed? The Greek view was that history is cyclical, like the seasons of the year. The Eastern view is that history is an illusion. The secular view is that history is a series of unconnected events without meaning. The Christian view is that history is headed toward an end time when Jesus will return and raise to everlasting life all who have believed. His return is something that he *promised* (John 14:3), that others *prophesied* (Heb. 9:28) and that all the creeds *confess*. When is Jesus coming back? Despite ongoing predictions, Jesus said, "only the Father" knows (Mark 13:32).

- **General Resurrection and Judgment.** At the end of the age there will be a *general resurrection* of all who have ever lived, and then a *final judgment*. What will the judgment be? For those who have believed in Jesus, it will be eternal life; for those who have not, it will be everlasting punishment. Some argue, however, that subjecting those who have never heard the gospel—children who die in infancy, those who are mentally disabled, those who live in closed societies or remote areas of the world—to eternal torment and suffering is inconsistent with a God of love and mercy. They believe that God must have some provision or Plan B for those who, through no fault of their own, have never had an opportunity to hear, understand and consider the gospel.
- **The Intermediate State.** What happens at death, and between death and the general resurrection? Regarding death, Christians hold different views. Some believe that both body and soul go to paradise, based on Jesus' statement to the thief on the cross:

85

"Today you will be with me in paradise" (Luke 23:43). Others believe that the soul separates from the body and lives on until the body is resurrected. Still others believe that we perish completely and then are resurrected. Catholics believe that those who die with unforgiven venial sins go to purgatory to have their souls purified. The period between death and final resurrection is called the intermediate state, about which the New Testament tells us, one writer said, "little more than a whisper." Theologians who hold that the soul continues to live on assume that it goes to a place that is permanent and eternal but incomplete until Jesus returns and gathers up all who have believed. Then, so the argument continues, the soul takes up residence in a new, resurrected body.

- **The Life Hereafter.** Theologian J. I. Packer says, "Heaven is shorthand for the Christian's final hope." Heaven is where the triune God "dwells"; it is also the dwelling place of the angels and of all the redeemed. What will life in heaven be like? One thing we know is that we will have new bodies, free from disease and decay (see 1 Cor. 15:35–44). Will we know those whom we love? The Apostles' Creed confesses the belief in "the communion of saints," the common bond of all believers in and through the Holy Spirit. The American theologian R. C. Sproul, in his book *Now, That's a Good Question!*, understands this to mean that we will be in fellowship with everyone who is "in Christ." What more can we say about heaven? Only that "No eye has seen, no ear has heard, no mind has conceived what God has prepared for those who love him" (1 Cor. 2:9 NIV). To say more is impossible because, as Louis Jacobs observed, "For human beings in this world to try to grasp the nature of the hereafter is like a man born blind trying to grasp the nature of color."

Angels, Satan and Demons

The modern world dismisses angels, Satan and demons as superstition and views those who believe in them as naive, but the Bible has much to say about them. Angels are mentioned in more than half the books of the Bible. What are angels, and what is their function? Angels are not physical beings but spirit beings; though they are created beings, they are immortal (Luke 20:34–36); and though often described in masculine terms, they are not sexual beings. Their purpose is to act as messengers of God—the word *angel* comes from a Greek word meaning "messenger"—as when the angel Gabriel spoke to Zechariah in the temple (Luke 1:11–20) and to Mary in Nazareth (Luke 1:26–38). Are angels still active? There is no scriptural warrant for believing that they were active only in biblical times. Are there such things as "guardian angels" that protect and preserve a believer's well-being? In Matthew's Gospel, Jesus tells the disciples not to despise one of these little ones because *"their angels* continually see the face of my Father in heaven" (Matt. 18:10, emphasis added). There is not much more than this, however, to go on.

Satan is not a "thing" but an active spirit being with an intellect and a will. His mission is to attack and oppose the people of God—the word *Satan* comes from a Hebrew word meaning "to oppose"—tempting them, as he did Jesus in the wilderness, to follow him and his evil ways. C. S. Lewis said that some people take the devil too seriously, while others don't take him seriously enough.

Demons are Satan's agents, as angels are God's agents. In the New Testament demons are often referred to as "unclean spirits," as in the Gospel of Mark, where Jesus rebuked an unclean spirit that possessed a man in a synagogue in Capernaum where Jesus was teaching (Mark 1:23–27).

8

OTHER RELIGIONS AND BELIEFS

Today there is a great movement of people to the West. Some come to start a new life, others to be reunited with relatives who came before, still others to study in colleges and universities. When they come, they bring religious beliefs that most Christians know very little about. In this chapter we will look at other world religions and belief systems and compare them with Christianity.

Hinduism: The Religion of India

Hinduism, which dates back to the second millennium before Christ, is the religion of India: 85 percent of all Indians are Hindus. The number of Hindus is estimated to be 810 million, making Hinduism the third largest religion in the world, after Christianity and Islam. Hinduism had no founding father and has no institutional form; though it has temples, it has no corporate or formal day of worship; and it believes there are thousands of gods. A dark side of Hinduism is the caste system of social stratification, which dates back to the 1500s when the Aryans (Indo-Europeans) invaded India. There are four primary castes and thousands of subcastes, which are hereditary and for life: one cannot move from one caste to another. One who has no caste is an "outcaste."

Hindus believe that the human soul, called *atman*, is linked with the universal soul, called *Brahman*. One's state in life is determined by one's *karma*, from a Sanskrit word meaning "actions." Bad karma leads to the reincarnation of the soul into lower orders (animals, plants and insects); good karma into higher orders (higher castes). The goal of Hindus is to secure the release of their atman from the endless repetition of births, deaths and rebirths and merge it with Brahman, like a drop of water falling into an ocean. A Western form of Hinduism is Hare Krishna—*Hare* means "lord" and *Krishna* is the *avatar* ("divine manifestation") of Vishnu, one of the three principal deities in Hinduism. Hare Krishnas believe in karma and reincarnation, but they do not believe in a plurality or pantheon of gods or in the caste system.

Buddhism: The Middle Way

Buddhism is another nontheistic Eastern religion. It was founded by Siddhārtha Gautama, who was born in 566 B.C. in what is now Nepal. According to Gautama, the cause of suffering is desiring and craving things that are worldly and temporal. The way to peace and serenity is the *Middle Way* of moderation between pleasure and denial, between indulgence and asceticism. Gautama became known as *Buddha*, a Sanskrit word meaning one who has attained "enlightenment." He taught that there is something one can do to escape the misery and suffering of this life, rather than waiting for a future life. What can one do? Adopt wisdom, morality and meditation as the essence of life and follow the *Noble Eightfold Path* of right views, aspirations, behavior, speech, livelihood, effort, mindfulness and contemplation. The Eightfold Path leads to *nirvana*—from a Sanskrit word meaning "to blow out" the flame of desire, the cause of suffering—and to the absorption of the finite self into the infinite, like a passing cloud that dissolves and disappears. A popular form of Buddhism in the West is Zen Buddhism. Zen adherents practice meditation according to strict rules in order to achieve enlightenment (called *satori*) more quickly than through traditional Buddhism, thus escaping the wheel of reincarnation. Today there are 360 million Buddhists, making Buddhism the fourth largest world religion.

Islam: Christianity's Greatest Competitor

Islam means "submission" to the will of *Allah*, the Arabic name for God. Islam is a large (1.2 billion), worldwide, rapidly growing, well-financed, missionary faith. It is the dominant religion and way of life in some sixty countries of the world, leading some to believe that the next global conflict will be between Islam and Christianity. We tend to think of Muslims as Arabs, but among the ten largest Islamic countries, only one (Egypt) is Arabic. Muslims worship in *mosques* ("place of prostration"), where the faithful—usually only men, at least in the main hall—gather together to pray as a group. The prayers are led by an *imam* ("he who stands before others"), a person with religious training, who delivers a sermon on Friday, Islam's day of formal worship (chosen, perhaps, to distinguish Islam from Judaism and Christianity). Most mosques have a minaret to call the faithful to worship, a fountain for ceremonial washing and education rooms for teaching the Koran and Islamic law.

Islam is divided into two major groups, the *Sunnis* and the *Shi'ites*. The Sunnis, with 85 percent of Islam's adherents, are the mainstream, but the Shi'ites—the more visible, vocal fundamentalists—are the more conspicuous. The Sunnis follow the *Sunna* (way or custom) of Muhammad and are led by *caliphs* (successors or representatives) from the Kuraish tribe, to which Muhammad belonged. The Shi'ites follow the line of Ali, Muhammad's cousin and son-in-law. They believe that Ali's descendants represent the true line of succession, which continues today in spiritual leaders like the *ayatollahs* ("sign of God") in Iran and elsewhere.

An African-American expression of Islam is the Nation of Islam, which was founded in 1931 in Detroit. Its adherents are known as Black Muslims. From the beginning, the NOI has been more interested in "blackness"—stemming from the days of Malcolm X, who preached black pride and black power in the 1950s—than in religion. Today there are 2–3 million Black Muslims in the United States. Most belong to orthodox Islamic communities, which the NOI is not.

- **The Prophet Muhammad.** The founder of Islam was Ubu'l-Kassim, who became known as *Muhammad*, the "Praised One." He was born in A.D. 570 in Mecca, an ancient city in present-day Saudi Arabia. When Muhammad was forty years old (in 610), he claimed to have had a vision of the angel Gabriel while meditating in a cave on Mount Hira, north of Mecca. Gabriel told Muhammad that he was

Allah's messenger and promised to dictate to him the word of God. Muhammad did not consider himself to be divine but the one chosen by God to be his final prophet—the "seal of the prophets." (There are twenty-five "prophets" in Islam, among whom are Jesus and John the Baptist.) Muhammad died in 632 at the age of 61. Following his death, Islam spread across North Africa and into Spain, challenging Christianity on its own soil.

- **The Koran.** In Islamic theology, God did not reveal himself in the form of a person, Jesus, but in words, which are recorded in the *Qur'an* or *Koran*, a word meaning "recitation." According to Islam, the recitations were revealed to Muhammad from 610 to 632 in Mecca and Medina, the two cities in which Muhammad lived. The recitations were given in manageable segments so they could be memorized. It is believed that Muhammad passed his "revelations" on to his secretary, Zayd, and they were later organized into a book by Uthman, the third caliph, around the year 650. The Koran has 114 *suras* or chapters, ordered by descending length rather than chronologically, which makes the Koranic story in places hard to follow. The Koran is slightly smaller than the New Testament.

- **Judaism, Christianity and Islam.** Judaism, Christianity and Islam are the world's three great monotheistic religions. All three look back to Abraham as their father, whom Islam believes was a Muslim because Muslims submit to the will of God and Abraham was the first person to do so. Also, Muslims believe that Ishmael, who was born fourteen years before Isaac, was the "promised son" and that it was he, not Isaac, whom God commanded Abraham to sacrifice on Mount Moriah. All three religions revere Jerusalem as a holy city, but for different reasons; in the case of Islam, because it was from Jerusalem that Muhammad made his famous "night journey" (in 620) to the seventh heaven, where Allah "resides." (The golden Dome of the Rock in Jerusalem was later built over the rock from which Muhammad allegedly ascended in order to memorialize the event.) And all three are People of the Book. Islam reveres the Torah, the book of Moses; the Psalms, the book of David; the Gospels, which it understands as biographies of Jesus, not good news, and in places has even rewritten (in the Koran, Jesus was born under a palm tree, not in a manger); and most important, the Koran. Muslims believe there is an exact copy of the Koran in Arabic in heaven.

Islam reveres Jesus and believes in his virgin birth and miracles and that before he died he was "assumed" into heaven, where he now resides with Allah. But Islam does not consider Jesus divine, because it would be unfitting for the sovereign God of the universe to become incarnate in a human being (in the Koran, Jesus is the Son of *Mary*, not the Son of *God*). Nor does Islam believe that Jesus was crucified, because Allah would not allow one of his prophets to die such a disgraceful, humiliating death (Islam believes that someone was crucified in Jesus' place, either Judas or Simon of Cyrene). Because Muslims believe that Jesus did not die, he was not, of course, raised from the dead.

Islam teaches that men and women are fundamentally good, not fallen. The fall in the Garden was caused by Satan, who tempted Adam (not Eve), who repented and was forgiven by Allah. Because humans are not fallen, there is no need for a Savior.

Muslims, though, have no present assurance of salvation: everything is on hold until the Day of Reckoning, when each person appears before Allah (not Jesus) to be judged by his or her deeds and works (salvation by works). Those judged faithful go to an oasislike paradise of unbelievable sensual pleasure; sinners go to a hell of indescribable punishment.

- **The Five Pillars.** There are five "pillars" that undergird Islamic religious life for observant Muslims. First, the profession that "there is no God but Allah, and Muhammad is his prophet." (Allah is not the knowable, personal God of Christianity; he is never described as a God of love, as in 1 John 4:16, or referred to as Father; and he is clearly not Trinitarian.) Second, prayers to Allah five times a day: upon rising, midday, midafternoon, sunset and upon retiring. When Muslims pray, they usually prostrate themselves in a position of humility. In public prayers, the words of the prayers come from the first chapter of the Koran and follow established formulas. Third, almsgiving, the sharing of one's wealth to support the sick and the needy. The amount varies, but the practice is 2.5 percent of a person's income or wealth. Fourth, abstaining from food and drink from sunrise to sunset during the month of Ramadan, the month it is claimed that Gabriel first appeared to Muhammad. Fifth, a pilgrimage to the Great Mosque in Mecca once during a Muslim's lifetime, if possible. Fundamentalist Muslims also believe in a sixth pillar, *Jihad*, meaning "spiritual struggle," one aspect of which involves waging war against enemies of Islam. Muslism who die in combat become martyrs and are assured of a place in paradise.

Christian Sects and Cults

A strong challenge to Christianity over the last 175 years has been the emergence of religious sects and cults that parade under the banner of Christianity but deny the central truth claims of Christianity. The word *cult* is a descriptive term, though some find it offensive, preferring instead the term "alternative religious movements." Historian Ruth Tucker, in her book *Another Gospel*, defines a cult as a religious group whose prophet/founder claims to have received a special revelation from God, set forth in the founder's "inspired" writings, to proclaim a message not found in the Bible. Tucker says that most cults have authoritarian leadership structures, are legalistic in lifestyle, are exclusivistic in outlook and have a persecution mentality.

- **Common Cult Beliefs.** The following are common cult beliefs regarding the central truth claims of Christianity. First, cults deny the Bible's authority, claiming it to be faulty and incomplete, which their founders have replaced with their own writings, such as Joseph Smith's *Book of Mormon*. Second, cults worship a god other than the biblical God, and each denies the Trinity (cults are unitarian rather than Trinitarian). Third, cults deny the divinity of Jesus, regarding him as human only, and none regard him as a savior. Fourth, cults do not believe in justification by faith; they believe instead in salvation by works, especially works on behalf of the cult, such as proselytization.
- **Popular Cults.** Four well-known cults were founded in the nineteenth century. The Church of Jesus Christ of Latter-day Saints (LDS), more popularly known as *Mormonism*, was established in 1830 by

Joseph Smith. The LDS has been called the most distinctive and successful religion ever born on American soil, with 11 million adherents worldwide. Mormonism believes in many gods; that the God who rules over our earth is a tangible being, not a spirit; and that "As man is, God once was; as God is, so man can become." Jehovah's Witnesses is the second-largest made-in-America religion, with 8 million adherents. It was founded in 1884 by Charles Taze Russell. Jehovah's Witnesses prefer the name *Jehovah* to God and believe that Jesus was the archangel Michael who laid down his spirit nature and became a man. They do not vote, pledge allegiance to the flag or sing the national anthem, nor do they celebrate Christian holidays or anyone's birthday. Christian Science was founded by Mary Baker Eddy in 1879. It is a philosophical system that believes in the superiority of spirit over matter; that God is the divine mind or principle of the universe; and that Jesus is the "Way-Shower" who revealed God as a spiritual principle. The Unity School of Christianity was founded by Charles and Myrtle Fillmore in 1889. Unity understands the Bible as an allegory and believes that God is a "principle" (of love); that Jesus was human only, not divine; and in reincarnation.

- **New Cults.** One of the newer cults is the Unification Church, founded by Sun Myung Moon in 1954. Moon claims to be the one chosen by God to redeem humankind. Two non-Christian cults—those that make no pretense of being Christian—are the Church of Scientology and Eckankar. Both believe in reincarnation. The New Age Movement is not a cult but a worldwide phenomenon that believes the present age is coming to an end, to be replaced by a "new age," the mythical Age of Aquarius. It believes in the interconnectedness of humanity, nature (Mother Earth) and the divine, called *monism* ("one-ism"), and in the law of karma and reincarnation. New Agers engage in channeling and other techniques to connect with the cosmic force or consciousness of the universe.

Do All Roads Lead to God?

In today's world of religious pluralism, Christians are in constant contact with people of different faiths. The question is often asked, "Do all religions lead to God?" The answer is that religions and beliefs such as those above may lead to "a" god, but not to the knowable, loving, triune God of Christianity. It has been said that the difference between Christianity and all other religions can be boiled down to the difference between *doing* and *done*. In all other religions, salvation comes through "doing" something. In Christianity, everything necessary for salvation has already been "done" by Jesus on the cross. As Christians, all we have to do is accept the *done-ness*.

9

GROWING IN AND SHARING CHRIST

As Christians, we are called to "pray without ceasing" (1 Thess. 5:17), to be transformed through the discipline of study (Rom. 12:2), to be ambassadors for Christ (2 Cor. 5:20) and to always be willing to share with others the hope we have in Jesus Christ (1 Peter 3:15).

Growing in Christ through Prayer

Surveys indicate that a major reason Christians shy away from sharing their faith is that they have, or believe they have, an impoverished faith. How can we make our faith strong and vibrant? Quaker writer Elton Trueblood, in *A Place to Stand*, says, "The three areas that must be cultivated [to build a strong faith] are the inner life of devotion, the intellectual life of rational thought and the outer life of human service."

- **The Life of Prayer.** Polls indicate that a majority of Christians are dissatisfied with their prayer life, and this includes clergy as well as laypeople. One reason is that in our busy-busy world we find it difficult to be quiet before the Lord—to sit and "wait upon the Lord." The Westminster Catechism of 1647 asks, "What is the chief end of man?" The answer is: "To glorify God and enjoy him forever." We glorify God when we come to him in prayer; we enjoy God when we bask in his presence, like a child sitting on the lap of a parent. Brother Lawrence, a seventeenth-century French Carmelite, believed that it was possible to "practice the presence of God." This phrase became the title of a book containing his writings that was published after his death.

- **Forms of Prayer.** There are three principal forms of prayer. Vocal prayers are *spoken* prayers. A helpful, widely used outline for verbal prayer is contained in the acronym ACTS, which stands for the *Adoration* of God, the *Confession* of sins and transgressions against God and others, *Thanksgiving* for God's blessings and promises and *Supplications* (petitions or requests) to God for special needs. God does not care about the correctness or beauty of our words, only that we come to him with a prayerful heart. Meditative prayer is praying with the *mind*, usually based on a passage of Scripture or a reading from a daily devotional. In meditative prayer, the pray-er meditates on the words before him or her. Contemplative prayer is the most advanced level of prayer. Contemplative prayer is hungering for a genuine "felt experience" of God, for hearing God's "still small voice," for union and intimacy with God. How do we do this? By quieting down, called *centering*—clearing the mind of all distractions—so that we can listen to God, who is everywhere present, like radio waves around us, waiting and wanting to speak to our minds and hearts.

- **The Lord's Prayer.** Jesus taught his disciples how to pray. The prayer that he taught them is called the Lord's Prayer (which is not Jesus' personal prayer because, among other things, it petitions God to "forgive us our sins," and Jesus was sinless). The Lord's Prayer has two parts or halves. The first part contains three supplications to God: that his *name*—not his name per se but his "essence"—be hallowed, honored, and reverenced; that his *kingdom*—his rule and reign over the earth—will soon come; and that his will be done—his will that we love him and others. The second part contains three petitions, which the Scottish commentator William Barclay said can be thought of as present, past and future. We pray for *today*—for our "daily bread," which includes shelter, medical care and other necessities of life. We pray for *yesterday*—for God's forgiveness when we have failed to love him and others around us. (We don't confess these things to tell God something he doesn't already know; we confess them so they may be forgiven.) And we pray for *tomorrow*—for God to be present when we are tempted (see 1 Cor. 10:13). Being tempted is not a sin; everyone is tempted. It is *yielding* to temptation that is sin.

- **The Practice of Prayer.** We do not learn how to pray by reading books on prayer; we learn by

101

engaging in the discipline of prayer. The following are some suggestions from people who have an active, daily prayer life. First, dedicate a certain time each day to being alone with God, perhaps first thing in the morning before our minds begin racing with all the tasks we have to do. Second, find a quiet place, with few distractions. Get comfortable, light a candle to remind you of Christ's presence and center your mind on God. Third, keep a spiritual diary to record thoughts and reflections that come to you during these times. Last, though prayer is an attitude, not a formula, structure is sometimes helpful. Another acronym for prayer is the word **PRAY.** *P* stands for *praise*—praising God for his goodness, for our faith and for those whom we love and who love us. *R* stands for *reflect*—reflecting on verses in Scripture or readings in a devotional as they come into our minds. *A* stands for *ask*—asking or petitioning God for personal needs and for the needs of others. *Y* stands for *yearn*—yearning to be "at one" with God, for intimacy with God, to be more in love with God. Another "help" to prayer is a daily devotional, such as Oswald Chambers' *My Utmost for His Highest*.

- **Answers to Prayer.** What about answers to prayer requests and petitions? Some prayers are answered immediately; others require persistence; and sometimes the answer is no, as in Paul's prayer to God to remove the thorn in his flesh (2 Cor. 12:7–10). God hears all prayers; we don't know why he *seems* to answer some (to our satisfaction) and not others. Some say the real issue, though, is not too few answers but too few prayers.

Growing in Christ through Study and Service

Prayer is the inward or interior life of Christian growth. Next, we need to study to make the Jesus of our heart the Jesus of our mind, and then let our faith issue forth in works of service. Study will help us give an answer to those who ask about the hope we have in Jesus (1 Peter 3:15). Service will let others see how this hope expresses itself in the good works spoken of by Paul in his letter to the Ephesians (2:10) and by James (2:14–26).

- **Growing in Christ through Study.** God wants us to grow in knowledge—to "be transformed by the renewing of [our] minds" (Rom. 12:2). The following are some suggestions for reading the Bible. First, get a Bible in a modern translation, preferably a good *study* Bible. Start with small, digestible doses of Scripture, reading slowly and carefully and asking what the meaning of the passage was to those to whom it was addressed (you will need a study Bible or a Bible commentary to do this) and what it means today. Second, be *consistent*. Get into the habit of reading the Bible every day. Third, be *systematic*. Stay with something and see it through to the end, rather than jumping from one book of the Bible to another. A good place to begin would be with one of the four Gospels, perhaps Luke because of the orderliness and completeness of his narrative. There are more than one hundred literary units (stories, parables and sayings) in Luke's Gospel; if you read one every day, Dr. Luke will keep you busy for months. Last, find ways to *apply* the Bible's teachings to your life. The purpose of Bible study is not information but *transformation*.

- **Growing in Christ through Service.** Christians are the best argument for Christianity—and also the worst. We are at our worst when we fail to reflect in our daily lives the one we profess as Lord and Savior. If we want others to consider the person, claims and promises of Jesus, we need to be the further incarnation of his message and teachings. How should we do this? Jesus tells us, in the story of the sheep and the goats (Matt. 25:31–45), that we are to feed the hungry, clothe the naked, care for the sick and visit the incarcerated. We also need to champion social justice, speak up and out against immorality, care for the environment and show Christian kindness to everyone who crosses our path.

Christian Apologetics

The defense of Christianity is called *apologetics*, which does not mean making an apology, as the name might suggest. Rather, it means giving reasoned answers to those who challenge the beliefs of Christianity—those whose naturalist worldviews do not allow for the possibility of a *super*natural, transcendent being; those who ask why there is evil and suffering in the world if God is all-powerful and all-loving; those who cannot bring themselves to believe in the incarnation and in Jesus' resurrection and miracles.

- **The Existence of God.** It is said that there are two "tracks" to God, one by way of nature, the other by way of revelation—the "works" of God in the world and the "words" of God in Scripture. *Natural theology* teaches that it is possible to come to the knowledge of God by reflecting on the world around us, which cannot be explained in terms of a random accident of nature. The other "track" is Scripture, which is called *revealed theology*. If there is a Creator, it seems natural that he would want to reveal his love for us and his will for our lives. How did God do this? By calling prophets and apostles to speak and record his Word so that one day all the world would come to know him. It is said that natural theology tells us of God's *creating* will and revealed theology of his *saving* will. There is also a third way that we know God: through the inner witness of the Holy Spirit. There are things that we know are true even though we cannot *prove* them. Right now I am working at my word processor, and I am hungry and thinking about lunch. I cannot "prove" that this is what I am thinking, or even that I am hungry—but I *know* these things are true, and I know that God is true, even though I cannot "prove" this.

- **Evil and Suffering.** There are no satisfactory answers to suffering, especially undeserved suffering, other than to say that free-will human beings often make bad decisions and choices, which result in personal suffering and also in the suffering of others. The good news is that suffering is not the end of the story. Joni Eareckson Tada was injured in a diving accident in 1967, when she was a teenager, leaving her paralyzed from the neck down. Joni said the thing that helped her most was to know that "one day I would have a body that worked, hands that could hug, feet that would run. It gave me a great deal of comfort to know that I had not been left alone, that God would give me a new body beyond the grave." As Paul told the Corinthians, God has prepared something wonderful and beautiful for those who love him (1 Cor. 2:9).

105

- **Jesus' Incarnation and Resurrection.** Non-believers reject the incarnation and the resurrection because neither can be understood in human terms. But many things cannot be understood in human terms. Take the brain, for example. No one can explain how the wiring in the brain allows us to reason, dream, remember the past, create works of art and enjoy vivid colors and fragrant aromas. Just because we cannot explain *how* Jesus was conceived and resurrected does not mean that these two "miracles" did not occur. As for Jesus' miracles in the Gospels, C. S. Lewis said, "Who, after swallowing the camel of the resurrection, can strain at such gnats as the feeding of the multitudes."

The Message of Evangelism: Jesus Christ

Jesus asked his disciples, "Who do people say that I am?" (Mark 8:27). What about today? *Cynics* say that Jesus was an imposter, claiming to be someone (the Son of God) whom he was not. *Skeptics* say that Jesus was a man about whom his followers developed a legend after his death. *Believers* say that Jesus was and is the incarnate, still-living Son of the God of the universe.

At the end of the day, though, we always come back to the resurrection, about which the following can be said. First, fifty days after Jesus' death, his disciples declared on the streets of Jerusalem that he had been raised from the dead (see Acts 2:22–32). If the Jews had wished to dispute this, they would have needed only to go to the family tomb of Joseph of Arimathea and produce Jesus' corpse, which in the dry Palestinian climate would not have decomposed; this would have ended everything. But there is no record of anyone coming forward to say that Jesus' body was still in the tomb or that it had been stolen. Second, if Jesus had not been raised, there would be no Gospels, no New Testament and no church. Why? Because a dead, still-in-the-tomb savior would not have been "good news." Third, many of those who publicly testified to Jesus' resurrection were imprisoned, nailed to crosses, thrown to the lions and burned at the stake. What gave them the strength to endure in the face of persecution, rather than renounce their faith that Jesus had been raised from the dead? The believable oral and written testimony of those who had seen the risen Christ.

The Mechanics of Evangelism: Sharing the Good News

It is often said that God has a *plan* for our lives. It would be more accurate to say that God has a *purpose* for our lives: to know Jesus Christ and to make him known to others. The following are some suggestions for making him "known" to others. First, begin where the other person is and ask about his or her beliefs. This often leads to him or her asking in return, "What do you believe?" which opens the door for you to share the unique, distinctive beliefs of Christianity.

Second, focus on the central message, which is having a personal relationship with God through Jesus Christ. Don't get sidetracked trying to explain the mysteries of the faith; or the lifestyles and acts of other Christians, even church leaders (our trust is in Jesus, not in fallen humanity); or why there is evil and suffering in the world. Keep to your beliefs and faith and what they mean to you and for your life—that Christ has given you something to live *for* (his promises) and something to live *by* (his teachings).

Third, avoid using Christian in-talk about the Bible being "the inspired Word of God" or being saved "by the blood (or cross) of Jesus" or being "justified by grace through faith" or the need to be "born again."

Fourth, do not judge other religions as false, and avoid making claims about Jesus being superior to the founders of other religions. This allows open discussion to take place, and dialogue is always more effective and productive than argument.

Last, remember that our role as witnesses is to be *presenters*, not persuaders. We are to present the Good News of Jesus as lovingly as possible—and then let the inner witness of the Holy Spirit work in the hearts and minds of those with whom we have shared the gospel.

Pascal's Wager

The French physicist Blaise Pascal died in 1662. His thoughts on religion were published after his death under the title *Pensées* (French for "thoughts"), which has become a Christian classic. One of the best-known sections in *Pensées* is Pascal's "wager." We all make a wager or bet on God, whether we know it or not. Pascal said that if we bet on God and there is a God, we *win* everything; if we bet on God and there is no God, we lose *nothing* because there is nothing to lose; if we bet against God and there is a God, we lose *everything*. In the end, the wager comes down to betting everything on Jesus as Lord and Savior.

10

LIVING CHRISTIANLY
IN THE WORLD

There is another challenge that is harder to answer than the existence of God, evil and suffering, and Jesus' resurrection and miracles. It is the failure of Christians to reflect their faith in their everyday lives. Christian theologian Os Guinness said, "The problem with most Christians is not that they aren't *where* they should be; the problem is that they're not *what* they should be right where they are." Being a Christian does not mean assenting to certain beliefs, like the Apostles' Creed; or being upright in character and following the Golden Rule; or being baptized and attending church services. Being a Christian means having a personal relationship with Jesus Christ and being the further incarnation of his message and teachings.

The Ten Commandments: Rules for Christian Living

Israel was called to be God's "light to the nations" (Isa. 42:6), something that would draw people to God. How was Israel to be such a people? By observing the commandments God gave to Moses on Mount Sinai, contained in the books of Exodus (20:3–17) and Deuteronomy (5:7–21). Jesus affirms the commandments in his dialogue with the rich young man (Mark 10:19), and the apostle Paul does so in his letter to the Romans (13:9).

Many people read the Ten Commandments as a series of narrow *shall nots*. Pastor James Moore, in his book *When All Else Fails . . . Read the Instructions*, says, "The Ten Commandments tell us how things work, how life holds together, how God meant things to be. Anyone who is awake enough to 'smell the coffee' can easily see that life is better when we love God and other people . . . when we respect our parents and tell the truth . . . when we are honest and faithful in all of our relationships."

1. **You shall have no other gods before me.** The word "gods" refers to the fact that there were many gods in the ancient world. Today we do not think in terms of a plurality of "gods," but we do worship other gods—reputation, success, wealth, power, pleasure. After filming *The Ten Commandments*, Cecil B. DeMille was asked which commandment he thought people break the most. DeMille said, "The first one. It is the one Israel broke first and the one we still break most often." We are called to love God with our heart, soul, mind and strength (Deut. 6:5 and Mark 12:30), which means giving God *first priority* in our lives.

110

2. **You shall not make for yourself an idol.** God told Moses, "I AM WHO I AM" (Exod. 3:14). God spoke but was not seen. For this reason no graven (sculpted, carved or chiseled) image was possible. Today we don't make idols of God, but we do *idolize* others—royalty, rock musicians, movie and television stars, professional athletes, fashion models—until they burn out and fade away. We are called to worship God and *God alone*.

3. **You shall not misuse the name of the Lord your God.** The word *God* does not mean the *name* of God—which was so sacred that it was never audibly uttered in ancient Israel—but the *essence* of God. Today this commandment refers primarily to language that profanes God in speech, jokes, writings and graffiti. To avoid profaning God's name, we use euphemisms like Gosh (God), Jeez (Jesus) and Cripes (Christ) to profane things that are holy without mentioning them by name. We are to take God's name in *earnest*, not in vain, as we pray in the Lord's Prayer: "Hallowed be thy name."

4. **Remember the Sabbath day by keeping it holy.** God rested on the seventh day so that he could enjoy his creation; the Israelites rested on the seventh day so that they could enjoy God. Today Sunday has moved from a holy day to a holiday. We honor this commandment by keeping Sunday *holy*, by being part of a worshipping community, by reaching out to those who need a "God-touch" in their lives.

5. **Honor your father and your mother.** The remaining six commandments have to do with our relationships with others—our parents, our spouse and our neighbors. Today we have a diminished view of the family, and also the elderly (we admire youth and youthfulness, not old age). We need to

care for those who have no family—those for whom we can *become* family—showing the kind of hospitality Jesus referred to when he said, in the story of the sheep and the goats, "I was a stranger and you invited me in" (Matt. 25:35 NIV).

6. **You shall not murder.** This commandment has to do with the *sanctity of life*. It has been broadened to include any form of killing and furnishes the biblical basis for those who oppose capital punishment, war, euthanasia, even recruitment into the armed forces. It also furnishes the basis for those who say that aborting an embryo is killing one made in the image of God (Gen. 1:26).

7. **You shall not commit adultery.** This commandment protects the institution of *marriage*, in which God joins man and woman together to become "one flesh" (Gen. 2:24 and Mark 10:6–9). Many feel that the sexual revolution that began in the 1960s, which continues today in the widespread liberalization of sexual mores and values, has been responsible for the breakdown of the family unit.

8. **You shall not steal.** This commandment has to do with *honesty*. In its broadest form, it deals with the misappropriation of funds and property, the manipulation of others through bribery and payoffs and the falsification of reports and records.

9. **You shall not give false testimony against your neighbor.** This commandment has to do with *truthfulness*. It includes perjury, slander, libel and gossip—in fact, the protection of another person's reputation against any form of false witness, even remaining silent when a person is being wrongly slandered. We need to tell "the whole truth and nothing but the truth."

10. **You shall not covet.** The final commandment is a prohibition against desiring and lusting after status and success, wealth and possessions, health and youthfulness, and pleasure in all its physical forms. Coveting is one of the seven deadly sins, that of envy. How do we control covetousness? By practicing its opposite, which is *contentedness*.

The Ten Commandments Today

Television journalist Ted Koppel, in a speech to the graduating class at Duke University in 1987, said that Moses came down from Mount Sinai with Ten *Commandments*, not Ten *Suggestions*. "The sheer beauty of the Commandments," Koppel said, "is that they codify in a handful of words acceptable human behavior, not just for then or now but for all time."

The Sermon on the Mount: The Christian Manifesto

There are two so-called *sermons* in the Gospels: Matthew's Sermon on the *Mount* (Matt. 5:1–7:29) and Luke's Sermon on the *Plain* (Luke 6:17–49). Matthew's Sermon on the Mount is the more familiar of the two; it is presented as a single piece, but many believe it is a summary of Jesus' teachings because of its length and complexity and because there is a different placement of the various passages in Luke's Gospel. On which "mount" the sermon was preached is not known, but in the Bible *mounts* are places where God has spoken and revealed himself. Examples include Mount Moriah (where Isaac was taken to be sacrificed), Mount Sinai, Mount Carmel (where Elijah battled the prophets of Baal), the Mount of Transfiguration and Mount Zion, where the psalmist says God "resides" (Ps. 48:1–2).

The Beatitudes

The Sermon on the Mount opens with eight Beatitudes or Blesseds—eight qualities that should be seen in the lives of Christians, like Paul's nine fruits of the Spirit in Galatians 5. Some have conjectured that the Beatitudes are the "bottom lines" of sermons that Jesus preached time and again throughout Galilee, which Matthew has brilliantly summarized into a series of eight teachings.

1. **Blessed are the poor in spirit.** Blessed are those who realize that they are helpless to save themselves, those who put their total trust and hope in God, those who wager everything on the grace and mercy of God. Peter said to Jesus, "Lord, to whom can we go? You [alone] have the words of eternal life" (John 6:68).
2. **Blessed are those who mourn.** Blessed are those who grieve over the cruelty and pains of the world, those who are moved by the sufferings of others and offer them comfort rather than passing by, like the Good Samaritan, who came to the aid of the man beaten by robbers on the road to Jericho (Luke 10:25–37).
3. **Blessed are the meek.** Blessed are those who are gentle, loving and compassionate, those who are willing to humble themselves before others, like the father who humbled himself before his wasteful younger son and his angry older son in the parable of the prodigal son (Luke 15:11–31).
4. **Blessed are those who hunger and thirst for righteousness.** Blessed are those who hunger to be right with God, those who thirst after his will,

those who desire to be upright and righteous in his sight. Amos told the Israelites that God does not want false worship; he wants to see "justice roll on like a river, righteousness like a never-failing stream" (Amos 5:24 NIV).

5. **Blessed are the merciful.** Blessed are those who do not repay evil with evil but with love, those who show kindness and mercy to all, those who are willing to forgive and forget grievances against them, as Jesus did on the cross: "Father, forgive them, for they do not know what they are doing" (Luke 23:34 NIV).

6. **Blessed are the pure in heart.** Blessed are those whose motives are true and genuine, those who pray for an inner purity of heart, as David did after his affair with Bathsheba, when he prayed: "Create in me a pure heart, O God, and renew a steadfast spirit within me" (Ps. 51:10 NIV).

7. **Blessed are the peacemakers.** Blessed are those who strive for peace and for right relationships, those who are peacemakers between persons at enmity with one another, those like Saint Francis of Assisi, who prayed, "Lord, make me an instrument of your peace."

8. **Blessed are those who are persecuted for righteousness' sake.** Blessed are those who speak out against social and political injustice and those who are willing to defend Christ's name before others. Jesus said that those who suffer for his sake and stand "firm to the end will be saved" (Mark 13:13).

Jesus' Other Teachings

Jesus' other teachings in the sermon have to do with being salt and light in the world; the six antitheses ("You have heard it said . . . , but I say . . ."); prayer and fasting; the error of seeing the speck in another's eye but not the plank in our own; asking, seeking and knocking, for God wishes to "give good gifts to those who ask him"; the impossibility of serving two masters (God and wealth); seeking first the kingdom of God and his righteousness; the so-called Golden Rule; and the narrow gate, the good tree and the strong, well-built house.

The Sermon on the Mount Today

How can we live out the Sermon on the Mount? One way is to keep our focus on the preacher of the sermon, namely, Jesus. Charles Blondin, the French tightrope walker, crossed over Niagara Falls several times in the summer of 1859. When he was asked how he did it, Blondin said, "I keep my eyes on an object on the far side of the falls and never look away." How can we live the Sermon on the Mount? By keeping our eyes on Jesus.

Jesus' Parables

There are some forty-five parables in the Gospels, all of which appear in the first three Gospels (John uses discourses rather than parables). The German scholar Joachim Jeremias said that all of Jesus' parables are unique. When we read or hear them, Jeremias said, we encounter Jesus "face to face."

- **The Good Samaritan** (Luke 10:25–37). The Good Samaritan is perhaps Jesus' best known parable. We refer to the Samaritan as *good*, but he is not called "good" in the parable. This is a later inter-pretation, one that has made its way into everyday usage, even into the media with reports such as,

116

"Today a Good Samaritan rescued . . ." A "lawyer" (an expert in the law of Moses) asked Jesus what he must do to inherit eternal life. The lawyer understood the two great commandments—to love God (Deut. 6:5) and to love one's neighbor (Lev. 19:18). What he didn't understand was that a neighbor was *anyone in need*. In the parable, the priest and the Levite are more interested in keeping the law—not touching the fallen man, who might have defiled them—than in showing love and mercy to someone in need. The Good Samaritan was and is the perfect example of loving one's neighbor. He did something that was totally unexpected—coming to the aid of a Jew (Jews and Samaritans had no relations with each other, according to John 4:9); he acted spontaneously, without worrying or wondering what he should do; and he did more than the minimum—he treated the man's wounds, he transported the man to the inn and paid for his care, and he agreed to pay more if more was needed. The parable of the Good Samaritan presents a problem: are we to care for everyone who crosses our path? If not, where do we draw the line? Jesus' command to love one's neighbor is a universal command; it is not limited to those who are easy or convenient to love. Today, in Israel, it might mean a Jew showing love to a Palestinian or vice versa; in the United States, it might mean showing love to someone from the Middle East or someone who is gay or someone with HIV.

- **The Rich Man and Lazarus** (Luke 16:19–31). The parable of the rich man and the beggar Lazarus (not to be confused with the Lazarus in John's Gospel), who sat at the rich man's gate waiting for a crumb, is one of many parables in Luke about the proper use of one's wealth. The poor man died and was carried away by angels; the rich man died and went to Hades (the "netherland" between heaven and hell). Why the switch? Because the rich man ignored the poor man at his gate, and in so doing he ignored God as well. The apostle John echoes the teaching of this parable, saying, "If anyone has material possessions and sees his brother in need but has no pity on him, how can the love of God be in him?" (1 John 3:17). One day we will be called to account for the gifts and blessings we have received—and our treatment of those at our gate.

Habits of Godly Living

The year 1989 saw the publication of Stephen Covey's national bestseller *The Seven Habits of Highly Effective People*. How can we live out and give witness to our Christian faith in today's world? One way would be to develop "Seven Habits of Godly Living" from the second tablet commandments (five through ten), Jesus' Beatitudes and antitheses in the Sermon on the Mount, Paul's fruit of the Spirit in his letter to the Galatians (5:22–23), Paul's virtues in his letter to the Colossians (3:12–15) and Paul's teachings on Christian behavior in Romans (12:9–21). From these and other texts, we can develop personal, tailor-made "Habits of Godly Living" to guide us in living Christianly in our homes, neighborhoods and places of work, and in our recreation and leisure.

═╣JUDEO-CHRISTIAN TIMELINE╠═

2000 B.C.–A.D. 2000

B.C.

(also referred to as BCE: Before the Common Era)

2000 God's call of Abraham to "Go to the land that I will show you" (Gen. 12:1 NIV)

1290 Moses leads the Israelites in their exodus out of Egypt

1250 Joshua leads the Israelites into Canaan, the Promised Land

1000 The beginning of the reign of King David, Israel's most important king

587 The destruction of Jerusalem and the Judean exile in Babylon

538 The return of the exiles and the rebuilding of Jerusalem

332 Alexander the Great invades and conquers the land of Palestine

164 The Maccabean uprising and the rededication of the temple (*Hanukkah*)

63 The Roman army invades and occupies Palestine

37 Herod the Great becomes the king of the Jews

6 Jesus of Nazareth is born in Bethlehem

A.D.

(Anno Domini, "in the year of our Lord"; also referred to as CE)

30 Jesus' death, resurrection and ascension

33 The call and conversion of Paul on the road to Damascus

70 The Gospel of Mark: the earliest of the four canonical Gospels

312 The conversion of Constantine: the first Christian Roman emperor

325 The Council of Nicea formulates the Nicene Creed

380 Christianity becomes the official religion of the Roman Empire

405 Jerome completes his translation of the Scriptures into Latin (the *Vulgate*)

1054 The church splits into Roman Catholic and Eastern Orthodox

1095 Pope Urban II launches the first crusade to recapture Jerusalem

1273 Aquinas completes the *Summa Theologica* (Summary of Theology)

1382 John Wycliffe translates the Latin *Vulgate* into English

1456 Johann Gutenberg invents the printing press

1492 Christopher Columbus opens the New World to the gospel

1517 Martin Luther's "Ninety-five Theses" launches the Protestant Reformation

1534 England separates from Rome and makes the king the head of the church

1536 John Calvin's *Institutes of the Christian Religion* systematizes Protestantism

1545 The Council of Trent: the Catholic response to the Reformation

1611 The *King James Bible* becomes the "authorized" Bible of Protestantism

1620 The *Mayflower* sails to the New World: "a colony for the glory of God"

1647 The Westminster Catechism: "to glorify God and enjoy him forever"

1793 William Carey begins Protestant missionary work in Calcutta

1906 The Azusa (Los Angeles) Street Mission: the birth of Pentecostalism

1947 The discovery of the Dead Sea Scrolls: the oldest Jewish manuscripts

1949 Billy Graham's first crusade in Los Angeles (210 million attendees to date)

1963 Pope John XIII calls Vatican II: the beginning of Catholic "modernism"

1991 The dissolution of the USSR and the reinstatement of religious freedoms

2000 Amsterdam 2000 issues *Amsterdam Declaration on Evangelism*

SUMMARY COMPARISON OF THE FOUR GOSPELS

	Mark	Matthew	Luke	John
Verses	661	1,068	1,149	878
Date	65–70	Mid-80s	Mid-80s	Mid-90s
Author	John Mark, a follower of Peter	Matthew, the disciple, or his followers	Luke, a companion of the apostle Paul	John, the disciple and apostle
Audience	Gentile Christians in Rome	Jewish Christians in Syria/Galilee	Christians in the Greco-Roman world	Christian community in Ephesus
Jesus' Mission	"To give his life a ransom for many " (10:45)	"To fulfill what had been spoken" (1:22)	"To seek out and to save the lost" (19:10)	To do "the will of him who sent me" (6:39)
Portrait of Jesus	Crucified Son of God	Promised Messiah	Universal Savior	The Word Incarnate
Beginning of the Jesus Story	Baptism by John the Baptist	Birth and Jewish genealogy	Birth and universal genealogy	Before Creation (the divine *logos*)

	Mark	Matthew	Luke	John
Jesus' First Important Public Act	Capernaum: Jesus' first healing (1:21–28)	Sea of Galilee: Jesus' first sermon (5–7)	Nazareth: Jesus' first self-claim (4:16–21)	Cana: Jesus' first sign (2:7–11)
Structural Centerpoint	Peter's confession of Jesus as the Messiah (8:27–31)	Peter's confession of Jesus as the Messiah (16:13–21)	Start of Jesus' journey to Jerusalem (9:51)	Jesus' washing the disciples' feet (13:1–11)
Unique Jesus Materials/ Stories in the Narrative	Jesus' action and urgency ("immediately"); Jesus' humanness; Jesus' miracles (one-third of Gospel); Jesus' passion (first written account)	Jesus as the fulfillment of Israel's hopes; Jesus' Sermon on the Mount; Jesus' "end-times" discourse (24–25); Jesus' Great Commission	Jesus' birth narrative; Jesus' concern for sinners, outcasts and women; Jesus' parables (most in number and most unique); Jesus' ascension	Jesus as "the Word made flesh"; Jesus' "born again" dialogue with Nicodemus; Jesus' seven signs; Jesus' seven "I am" sayings
Special Features	Earliest; shortest; straightforward; two endings	Pride of place; systematic; OT references and citations; catechetical	Historical; sophisticated; Holy Spirit; book of Acts is sequel	Independent of Synoptics; eyewitness; theological; most popular
Symbol	Lion	Man	Ox	Eagle

John Schwarz has academic degrees in business management and law and has spent his working life in the corporate business world. He also has a degree from Regent College, an international school of theology in Vancouver, British Columbia. Schwarz took early retirement and went to Africa, where he taught business classes in a Christian college, taught the Bible in an indigenous church and started a primary school in a large slum. Schwarz was raised an Episcopalian. As an adult, he and his wife and children were active members of a Congregational church; while in seminary, he and his wife attended a Plymouth Brethren chapel; when they lived in Nairobi, they worshipped in an indigenous Baptist church; today they are members of an inner-city Methodist church in Minneapolis in the summer and a suburban Presbyterian church in Scottsdale in the winter.

Your church or small group can experience
LIVING FAITH!

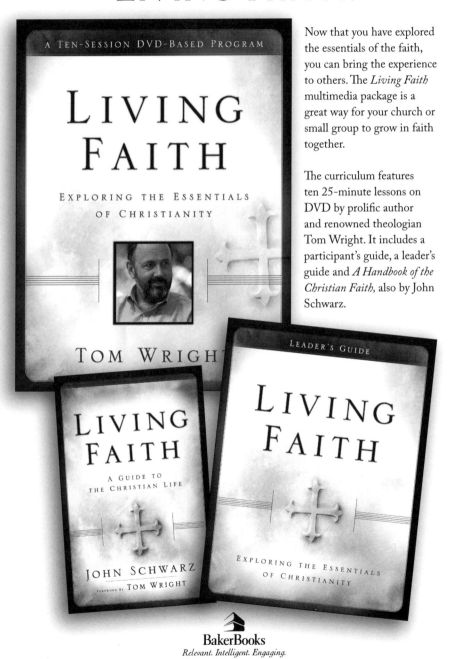

Now that you have explored the essentials of the faith, you can bring the experience to others. The *Living Faith* multimedia package is a great way for your church or small group to grow in faith together.

The curriculum features ten 25-minute lessons on DVD by prolific author and renowned theologian Tom Wright. It includes a participant's guide, a leader's guide and *A Handbook of the Christian Faith*, also by John Schwarz.

A TEN-SESSION DVD-BASED PROGRAM

LIVING FAITH

EXPLORING THE ESSENTIALS OF CHRISTIANITY

TOM WRIGHT

LIVING FAITH

A GUIDE TO THE CHRISTIAN LIFE

JOHN SCHWARZ
FOREWORD BY TOM WRIGHT

LEADER'S GUIDE

LIVING FAITH

EXPLORING THE ESSENTIALS OF CHRISTIANITY